Praise for *Branding Across Borders:*
A Guide to Global Brand Marketing

"Corporate Express will benefit from Branding Across Borders as we did with *Leveraging the Corporate Brand,* also written by James Gregory. Jim has a way of writing pertinent and clear information about branding so that it is useful to any business. We are excited about taking our North American brand platform and evolving it to a global brand platform that will be right for each of the twenty-two countries we operate in. This new book will be our guiding light."

VIKI MANN
Director, MarComm & Corporate Branding
Corporate Express, North American Headquarters

"Just when we thought we were beginning to understand branding, along comes Jim Gregory's new book reminding us that we're citizens of a global village. *Branding Across Borders* offers clear, concise, and thought-provoking ideas about the challenge of extending brands around the world. Yes, the book includes information about how to articulate your brand; but Jim also reminds us that it is equally important that global companies hear and understand the messages of other cultures."

ROD IRVIN, APR
Director, Communications Planning and Strategy
Eastman Chemical Company

"Jim Gregory has developed a well-deserved reputation as the global authority on corporate branding. Gregory doesn't just rest on his opinions; he has the database to back them up. No one can dispute that in virtually every market, companies must now learn to compete on a global basis, and that means building brands. Gregory now provides indispensable tools to help all of us do just that. All of us in the brand-building mode are in his debt."

THOMAS R. MARTIN
Senior Vice President, Director of Corporate Relations
ITT Industries

"We at Omron have first-hand experience in utilizing Jim Gregory's methods within our company. Corporate Branding's approach advocates understanding a business's heritage and culture before applying the branding craft. This has proven critical in building acceptance of our brand both internally and externally."

YOSHIO TATEISI
Representative Director and Chief Executive Officer
Omron Corporation

"Jim's latest book couldn't be timelier. Global branding is a complex challenge that no major corporation can dodge any longer. All of us in the global branding business can benefit from Jim's authoritative take on the subject."

FRANCIS B. HARRISON
Manager, Advertising Group
Ricoh Company, Ltd., Tokyo

"An orderly exposition of how to go about developing your brand globally. This is of great significance not only for European and American companies, but increasingly for pan-Latin American regional companies."

JOSE MACAYA
Country Manager
Russell Reynolds Associates
Argentina–Chile

BRANDING

ACROSS BORDERS

A GUIDE TO GLOBAL BRAND
MARKETING

BRANDING

ACROSS BORDERS

JAMES R. GREGORY
with Jack G. Wiechmann

McGraw-Hill

Chicago   New York   San Francisco   Lisbon   London   Madrid   Mexico City
Milan   New Delhi   San Juan   Seoul   Singapore   Sydney   Toronto

Library of Congress Cataloging-in-Publication Data

Gregory, James R.
    Branding across borders : a guide to global brand marketing / James R.
Gregory with Jack G. Wiechmann.
        p.   cm.
    Includes index.
    ISBN 0-658-00945-1
    1. Brand name products—Marketing.   I. Wiechmann, Jack G.   II. Title.

HD69.B7 .G74   2001
658.8'27—dc21   2001030841

McGraw-Hill

A Division of The **McGraw·Hill** *Companies*

1 2 3 4 5 6 7 8 9 0   LBM/LBM   0 9 8 7 6 5 4 3 2 1

ISBN 0-658-00945-1

This book was set in Sabon
Printed and bound by Lake Book Manufacturing

McGraw-Hill books are available at special quantity discounts to use as premiums and
sales promotions, or for use in corporate training programs. For more information, please
write to the Director of Special Sales, Professional Publishing, McGraw-Hill, Two Penn
Plaza, New York, NY 10121-2298. Or contact your local bookstore.

This book is printed on acid-free paper.

To Evelyn Gregory,
my wife and best friend

Contents

Foreword

IT WASN'T THAT MANY months ago that *Business Week* sponsored a global conference with 250 attendees. Of all the seminars we offered that day, Jim Gregory's "The Value of Branding" was the only one that enjoyed standing room only—all day long. It seemed that everybody wanted to be there and participate.

His brochures on the value of branding, which he created specifically for *Business Week*, were gobbled up, and long before day's end, I believe, none were left. I was truly impressed at this response to Jim's presentation. It was not only a great barometer of the value he offers, but a positive sign of the insatiable appetite executives have for his knowledge and data.

This new book by Jim Gregory, *Branding Across Borders: A Guide to Global Brand Marketing*, is the third volume in his trilogy on building the corporate brand. It covers in depth that current hot topic: global branding.

Global branding is a kind of universal truth. All companies, wherever they exist in the world, have brands and are involved, basically, with the same issues. They all face problems of local culture and language differences, governmental regulations, politics, and so forth.

This book investigates these subjects and many more. It fully outlines measures to be taken in building and managing a global brand, providing the reader with convenient lists of keys and other valuable guides. It covers, too, a good many of the various pitfalls to be avoided when a brand crosses national borders.

Nor is the new, wired world of the Internet forgotten in *Branding Across Borders*. The emergence of the E-customer and the task of communicating successfully in an interactive world are discussed in detail. Another chapter is devoted to the rash of megamergers we have been witnessing and their influence on globalization and global branding.

Perhaps of special interest are the whys and wherefores of the decline in power of certain well-known brands, and a chapter that focuses on the future of global branding, including some of Jim Gregory's own predictions.

From the beginning of our acquaintance, I have observed Jim's career with great interest and respect. Chairman and CEO of Corporate Branding, LLC, Jim is considered a leading pioneer in the field of corporate and global branding and is a frequent speaker before corporate groups and organizations.

Partnering with *Business Week*, Jim has addressed our conferences around the world. From Frankfurt, Tokyo, and Singapore to Seoul and New York, he always draws enthusiastic crowds and good reviews. He has also worked with *Business Week* in the preparation of numerous highly informative booklets, including the following titles: "The Impact of Advertising on Brand Momentum," "The Impact of Advertising on Brand Power," "The Impact of Advertising to the Financial Community," "Branding the Merger, Merging the Brands," and "Digital Branding."

The first volume in Jim's trilogy, *Marketing Corporate Image: The Company as Your Number One Product*, distills into communications terms everything that makes a company unique and important to its key constituencies. The second, *Leveraging the Corporate Brand*, describes the process of measuring communications effectiveness and shows how leading companies use integrated communications to attain corporate goals. Both have been reprinted in Japanese, sure evidence of growing international interest in the subject of corporate image and branding.

The globalized world is now with us. This new book reflects much of Jim Gregory's latest thinking and experience with its various issues, especially those of global branding. *Branding Across Borders* is not only informative, but, unlike so many other "business" books, it is highly readable.

Bill Kupper
President and Publisher
Business Week

Acknowledgments

THE AUTHOR SINCERELY APPRECIATES all the support and guidance given this project by our editor, Danielle Egan-Miller, at McGraw-Hill. Her patience, understanding, and encouragement contributed much to the undertaking.

I am also deeply grateful to the many companies, agencies, and consultants that have shared so much of their time and information for the preparation of this book. I am especially indebted to John Alden, Ronald E. Ferguson, John B. Frey, Patrick Gorman, Melissa Grant, Judith M. Guido, James P. Hamilton, Douglas Hyde, Clark Johnson, Rachel Kunz, Shelly Lazarus, Jane Mackie, Thomas R. Martin, Pat Masuda, David Reyes-Guerra, Teri Ross, Nancy Sheed, Remy Simon, Louis Slovinsky, Sybil Sosin, and Mindy L. Zimmerman.

Particular recognition belongs to our Corporate Branding staff—especially Debra J. Drobisch, Stefanie Kubanka, Bruno Santini, and Patty Toogood—and to our clients, whose loyalty, experience, and suggestions have meant so much. Nor should I overlook the many useful contributions of The Conference Board. Finally, my thanks and congratulations one more time to Jack G. Wiechmann, who has again put concepts and words on paper so well.

Introduction

SEEMINGLY SMALL EVENTS can impact the economic value of your corporate brand. As companies become more complex, as they reach out across borders or are inspired to become globalized through the Internet, it becomes increasingly difficult to protect and nurture the corporate brand. With so many companies "going global," I believe it is important to manage the corporate brand on a global scale.

In the 1960s, Marshall McLuhan coined the phrase "global village" in recognition that new technology and instantaneous communication had shrunken time and space, effectively converting diverse societies into a single world community. As this view has gained in credibility and acceptance with each passing year, so too has "global branding" become one of the hot buzzwords in marketing.

This book is about the strategic implications of all communications branding programs across the globe: from introducing a single product across a single border to the impact of global socioeconomic issues on your company to what you can do to build your corporate brand.

Walter Wriston, former chairman of Citicorp, colorfully summarized globalization as "suddenly meeting a person you never heard of, who comes from a place you can't locate on a map, and who's eating your lunch in your own hometown."[1]

It has also been said that a global enterprise operates not just in terms of global markets, but in global locations, with global ownership and employees, and global asset management.[2] One way to determine whether your company is truly global or only multinational is to apply certain measurements to your situation. If you are global, more than half your assets will be abroad, 40 to 60 percent of your people will be international, and 40 to 60 percent of your shareholders will be international. As a multinational organization, you may do business in many places, but as a global entity, everywhere is your home.

Global branding inspires a number of questions. For example: What does it take for a corporation to advance from a multinational to a global structure? What are the obstacles to global branding? What are the CEO's responsibilities for global branding? What part does the Internet play? Is a corporate brand transferable to the global marketing scene?

Simple answers remain elusive and sometimes illusory. It's the purpose of this book to examine the global mind-set, determine the drivers of corporate globalization, and, in particular, to demonstrate the strong relationship between successful global marketing and global branding.

Most corporate leaders acknowledge that globalization's freer trade promotes the flow of people and ideas across borders, as well as the movement of goods, services, and capital. Still, many are divided on its real relevance. Some call global marketing a salutary economic event, holding promises for the future. Others consider it a two-edged sword, as likely to ravage emerging economies as to reward globally market-dominant businesses.

Severe economic slumps—such as the recent one in Asia—reveal the vulnerabilities of global marketing and suggest that vital decisions must often be made on the basis of expediency regardless of consequence.

However you may define or value the concept of global branding, its real impact lies not so much in the present as in the perceived strength of its long-term potential.

Corporate leaders may hold a variety of opinions on globalization and its effect on their companies, but they cannot ignore either the many inherent opportunities or the potential hazards of global marketing. Failure to understand and prepare for global needs can only lead to surprises, and often to undesirable results.

Whether you subscribe to global branding or not, it is here to stay and will confer great power to marketers who master it. The prospect, as characterized by G. William Dauphinais and Colin Price, is one of "growing economic interdependence of countries worldwide through the increasing volume and variety of cross-border transactions . . . and also through the more rapid and widespread diffusion of technology. . . . [Globalization] is shaping a new epoch where the tempo and breadth of change in the international economy both alters the character of the multinational corporation and makes porous the economic frontiers of the state."[3]

The nature of the truly global corporation is still evolving. Most CEOs are only now discarding old, provincial mind-sets and values to seek new ways to make their companies react positively to local cultures and environments. At the same time they look to preserve the leverage of their corporate brand and realize their vision. What is happening is no less than the creation of a new pattern of corporate opportunities and interdependencies, along with strikingly new conditions and parameters for marketing success.

Like corporate branding, global branding is a broad subject. It is even more complex, however, because of the many cultural, political, and economic challenges involved. For the reader's convenience, this book approaches branding across borders from a variety of perspectives. Some of these are:

- Important steps in building a strong brand
- The impact of corporate brand investment on preference and sales
- Problems presented by diverse cultures
- Communicating the brand in an interactive world
- The effect of mergers and acquisitions on the brand
- Brands in decline
- The future of global branding

As you read this book, please remember that corporate business is subject to inevitable change. Nothing lasts forever. Companies change. Managements change. Products and markets change. Mergers, acquisitions, divestitures, and spin-offs continue unabated. There is also some lag time between manuscript completion and publication.

In preparing this book, I have done my best to keep information as current as research allows. But stuff does happen. I apologize in advance for any outdated facts you may find, and I trust they won't diminish the basic intention and message of the book.

James R. Gregory
Stamford, Connecticut

1

Managing the Global Brand

THROUGHOUT THE WORLD, many companies are in transition. Reasons vary, but two in particular emerge as prime forces in business change today: globalization and corporate branding.

Corporate branding does not necessarily involve globalization, of course, but successful global expansion almost always presumes the execution and communication of a well-devised global brand. In this book I will cover the many strategic implications of a global branding program, whether merely the introduction of a single product across a single border or the global impact of social and economic issues on a company.

Just what is a global brand? You are undoubtedly familiar with local brands, sold in parts of a domestic market; national brands, found throughout the domestic market; and pan-regional brands, sold in two or more countries. Global brands have a much greater geographic reach, being available in all major markets and most minor ones. What's more, they are perceived as being global by consumers. Like McDonald's, Coca-Cola, and Sony, global companies possess worldwide reputations and images.

Hot Topics

Globalization and global branding are hot topics that inspire as many questions as there are CEOs to ask them, perhaps more. For example: What is the greatest global challenge? Do language and cultural differences alter communication needs and techniques? Can a corporate brand that's been designed for domestic business suit the global marketplace? Who is primarily responsible for building the global brand and for managing it? Perhaps particularly pertinent: Is globalization going to help our business grow? In the following chapters, I will confront these and other questions raised by the development of globalization.

Although globalization is regarded as a recent development, it dates back at least 500 years to the advent of science and exploration, the adoption of modern applied mathematics, and the beginnings of modern banking. By the end of the nineteenth century, globalization really got under way, as technological breakthroughs like the telegraph, railroad, and steamship—soon to be followed by the automobile, airplane, and radio—shrank the globe and merged economies. Investment capital flowed across borders, and labor became increasingly mobile, with millions emigrating from Europe to North America, Australia, and parts of Latin America.

Today, globalization is transforming the world in ways never imagined a century ago. Some companies have operations in more than 100 countries, sell products in twice as many, and boast global revenues larger than the GDPs of many countries. Exploiting technological improvements in communications, the modern global company can move quickly, nimbly, and effectively when the need arises.

Just how far does global branding reach in the ever-changing marketplace? In a recent speech, Shelly Lazarus, chairman and CEO of Ogilvy Worldwide, said:

> When I talk about brand, I am not just talking about packages. I am not just talking about fast-moving consumer goods. . . . We're much beyond that now.
>
> Services are brands, too. American Express is a brand built on security, recognition, and service. Lloyd's of London, Singapore Airlines, are both strong brands. As soon as I say the name, do you feel something? You know something about them. As soon as I say the names and tell you they're bringing out a new product or service, you will already know what the product or service would be like.

Entertainment and media have become branded. The BBC and CNN are recognized around the world. Actually, when we did a study about CNN, we discovered that the farther away you are from home, the faster you put CNN on when you walk into a hotel room. . . .

Not just companies are focused on branding. People have become brands. Witness the global influence of Michael Jordan, Tiger Woods, Ralph Lauren, Giorgio Armani. Events are brands—the World Cup, the Super Bowl, and the Olympics. . . . Even countries are recognizing themselves as brands. Many of them have some sort of brand initiative under way.[1]

Drivers of Growth

Unilever, one of the largest of global conglomerates, in its efforts to increase profitability, has adopted a strategy of acquiring leading global and local brands. Most recently it has acquired Bestfoods, taking over such well-known brands as Knorr, Skippy, and Hellmann's. Earlier, Unilever acquired SlimFast and Ben & Jerry's.

Acquisition is not the only key to global growth. Companies like Nike have become global networks of manufacturers producing goods that bear a brand name. It's something franchisers have been doing for decades. More than 80 percent of McDonald's restaurants, for example, a worldwide chain of more than 25,000 restaurants, are independently owned, and all are united by a common brand.[2]

In today's high-technology, knowledge-based economy, the intangible asset of the global brand is considered an important driver of corporate value and growth. But despite the recognized significance of this asset, many companies still do a poor job of monitoring and measuring their performance in this area.

As companies move rapidly into fast-moving E-commerce terrain (see Chapters 6 and 7), brand building becomes even more crucial. Increasing numbers of dot-com startups have been investing millions of dollars, obtained from venture capitalists, in an attempt to build brands overnight.

Why? Two reasons. First, the Internet makes it so easy to enter that any dot-com that wants to create a serious market presence before its competitors do has only a narrow window of opportunity. Second, brand building on the Internet can be remarkably fast. Traditional corporations like Avon, Coca-Cola, and General Electric take decades to

A FULL COMMITMENT

Few companies can match the global success of United Parcel Service. The will to deliver on its promise was the key, says James P. Kelly, chairman and CEO of UPS: "Open trade has provided much of the opportunity to expand our business worldwide; we have addressed this opportunity in two distinct ways. First, we made a full commitment to globalize. Second, we have aggressively executed our global expansion."[3]

The UPS commitment to global expansion required large capital investments in powerful information technologies, many new facilities and vehicles, as well as deepening the personal commitment of its thousands of employees throughout the organization. Their collective skills, imagination, and teamwork have propelled the company's global transition.

Upgrading its information management capabilities to include twelve mainframes, 90,000 PCs, 80,000 handheld computers, and the world's most extensive cellular communications network, UPS is now regarded as one of the leading technology companies in the world.

Information about the package to be delivered is just as important to UPS as the package itself. The management of information on customer distribution is certainly one of the most critical services it can provide, for UPS believes that the leader in information management will be the leader in international package distribution.

Through a series of mergers, acquisitions, and joint ventures with established local carriers, UPS has grown from operations in only three countries as recently as 1985 to a network of more than 200 countries. CEO Kelly concedes that when the company first ventured outside the United States, it made some mistakes: "We thought we could go it alone, and applied our reliable domestic formula to new and different cultures. We learned an important lesson very quickly: Doing business globally is not simply a matter of grafting a rigid set of operations from one country to another. What works well in the Netherlands could easily fail in Italy and vice versa."[4]

build global brands, but it has taken as little as five years for Amazon .com to accomplish the same thing.

"Ultimately, brands are all about trust," Mukul Pandya writes in the *Wall Street Journal*. "The reason consumers flock to some brands and ignore others is that behind the brand stands an unspoken promise of value. That is why brands are becoming ever more important drivers of growth. That is also why Unilever wants Knorr, Skippy, Hellmann's, SlimFast, and Ben & Jerry's on its plate."[5]

Some Puzzling Dilemmas

The transition to a global presence can often pose puzzling dilemmas for management. One of the most common is to decentralize business decisions to meet the needs of the local marketplace while ensuring that the company brand is promoted via a globally consistent message in all forms of communication.

Moreover, the pressures of international competition, worldwide availability of technology, shifting markets, and increasingly mobile customer bases are forcing companies to review their structure and business practices from a global perspective. Companies going global are also called upon to rethink their corporate brands and implement changes needed to reflect global reality.

And as domestic and international markets expand into global markets, new local and/or regional competitors may emerge. These newcomers may often compete with an arsenal of lower labor costs, new manufacturing processes, and advanced technology applications. A continued development of technology not only creates early obsolescence of equipment and processes, but also speeds up the exchange of information and decision-making.

Rapid market growth in developing nations, along with slower growth in the more developed countries, forces businesses to seek expansion in unfamiliar territories. In addition, consumer audiences are now more savvy and realize they have a great many more choices.

The Value of the Brand

With this rapidly expanding and highly competitive global marketplace, there is a growing awareness of the significance of corporate and prod-

A CONFEDERATION OF COMPANIES

Avon Products bases its success on the "think globally, act locally" model. Edwina Woodbury, former executive vice president, noted that two-thirds of the company's business is outside the U.S. Avon has close to 50 operating companies in about 135 countries. Its culture and structure have been highly decentralized, making Avon, in effect, a confederation of companies that all do virtually the same thing around the world.

Woodbury points to three main challenges:

> We need to, and have the opportunity to, globalize most of our business processes, for purposes of increasing speed and efficiency, and, in many cases, achieving a more consistent image. We need to meet our customer where she is—in addition to our one-on-one sales approach, which means at retail or on-line or in direct mail, wherever a customer wants to buy Avon products, and to do that without disenfranchising our traditional Avon representative. We need to raise technology from the level of an enabler to a truly strategic lever for achieving linkage with our associates, sales force, and customers.[6]

To achieve these ends, the company launched a global process redesign effort, a key element of which is to transfer the ownership of the effort to local leaders. Rather than globalizing its approach, Avon gathered the learning, fed it back, and, within certain guidelines, continued to allow initiatives at the local and regional level, where they discovered most innovation comes from.

uct brands as strategic factors in building a company's value; not only at home, but globally as well. In fact, a company's brand often impacts stock performance by as much as 5 percent on average—a significant number that can make a major impression on market valuation. The brand is one of a company's most significant assets—an asset that, like any other of great value, requires constant, prudent management.

CEOs, directors, and senior managers expect the well-leveraged brand to offer a number of benefits. Research studies done by Corporate Branding show, among other things, that brand image contributes to positive corporate financial performance, affecting both share price and revenue. Thus, the brand serves as an attractive beacon for investors and the entire financial community. Obviously it also attracts customers.

The global brand's personality and style, along with its reputation for quality performance, help the customer differentiate company products from those of its competitors, and encourage customer loyalty in the process. Such a relationship is pivotal to a successful globalization effort.

In other words, branding grows customer recognition and loyalty. It boosts sales, helping to build and retain market share. In addition, it gives the manufacturer more leverage with retailers. The more consumers expect to be able to purchase a brand, the more difficult it becomes for the retailer not to carry it.

Studies also indicate that the introduction of new products and the opening up of new markets can be managed more efficiently with a recognizable and meaningful brand in place. And in today's highly competitive marketplace, brand preference can also help slow price erosion and even command a premium price.

Perhaps the most prevalent reason given for global branding is that of economy, particularly the economies achieved by an extended scope of sales driving down the average unit cost. And production-side savings are not the only economies realized. Marketing and advertising costs, as well, can be cut by concentrating spending against a single global brand instead of a number of brands.

Five Key Market Trends

In the 1990s the need for effectively managing the brand asset in an increasingly global marketplace has become apparent. There is a strong interest in global branding because of five key market trends:

- Rising economies of scale
- Exploitation of experience curves and knowledge transfers
- Capitalizing on geographic image spillover
- Seeking new growth opportunities
- Consolidation and globalization of the retail trade[7]

As global markets turn more competitive, it becomes more and more expensive for a company to achieve a meaningful marketplace advantage. Rising costs of research and development for product differentiation, along with production cost advantages that necessitate plant capacities that exceed local demand, call for companies to globalize their brands in order to amortize these and other costs across local markets.

As a firm competes in local markets, it learns through experience how to best create a viable brand position and how to mount successful brand advertising and promotional campaigns. Such knowledge may then be transferable to other markets. Some local brands gain global exposure without benefit of any active corporate support. To a great extent this is due to the ongoing spread of global communications—especially the Internet—greater international travel for both business and pleasure, and the globalization of the news and entertainment industries.

In order to achieve the revenue growth demanded today, many brands must enter new markets that offer either high growth opportunities or relatively weak competition. This is especially true of those mature brands with growth potential limited by national markets.

Another important trend is toward retail trade consolidation, often resulting in global megachains. These derive critical market advantages from sharing information and technology, refined logistic systems, and greater negotiation power over manufacturers.

Studies indicate there are four key steps crucial to effective global brand management:

First, focus on the various desired benefits to your company of being a global brand. Then determine the type of global brand that will yield those benefits, clearly marking which aspects of the brand are globally standardized and the acceptable range of local adaptation. Third, pay strict attention to historical legacies. The longer a company delays the costs associated with overcoming the past, the higher such costs become. And finally, match your organizational structure to the global brand strategy. Implications for the global-to-local relationship must always be considered, especially when determining where P&L responsibility resides.

There used to be only two ways of approaching the global branding process. One, the traditional headquarters approach; the other, a multilocal strategy, focusing on the special requirements of each and every marketing area. The first may be efficient, but is not particularly sensitive locally. The second is locally sensitive, but highly inefficient and not suitable for global branding.

Today, the technique that works best is what some call "transnational" or "glocal." Such an organization strives for global coverage and efficiency, but also respects local traditions and sensitivities and recognizes a need for market-by-market flexibility.

A Value-Added Tool

By differentiating products and services from those of competitors, a company is made less vulnerable to competitive marketing actions. When a brand clearly expresses a company's mission and values, it can also motivate employees and unite the organization in a common cause.

Caterpillar Inc., one of the world's most powerful corporate brands, makes a point of using branding as a value-added competitive tool. The $19 billion-a-year manufacturer of construction, mining, and agricultural machines has been able to introduce its famous industrial brand into consumer markets. In 1994, for example, Caterpillar began licensing its brand to a retail shoe manufacturer, and by 1997, 16 million shoes bearing the Caterpillar brand were sold in 109 countries.

Thus, Caterpillar has used established products strategically to control its brand definition and find creative new markets for it. Building on its record of acknowledged quality, the Caterpillar brand now transcends its products. It stands for strength, power, and progress, attributes that can be associated logically and easily with the trendy line of Cat walking shoes and other consumer products.

As Caterpillar knows, to excel, global corporations must have working partnerships with their customers as well as with suppliers and subsidiaries. Customers are never completely satisfied, and success with them depends on first-class communication. The customer's voice drives decisions, and planning must be well coordinated to ensure that his or her needs are met, if not exceeded.

But We Already Have a Brand!

What if your company already has a corporate brand? Do you need to improve or change it when you go global? This depends on many factors, but if the brand is successful and well-recognized, probably not.

Figure 1.1   *Footwear Catalog*

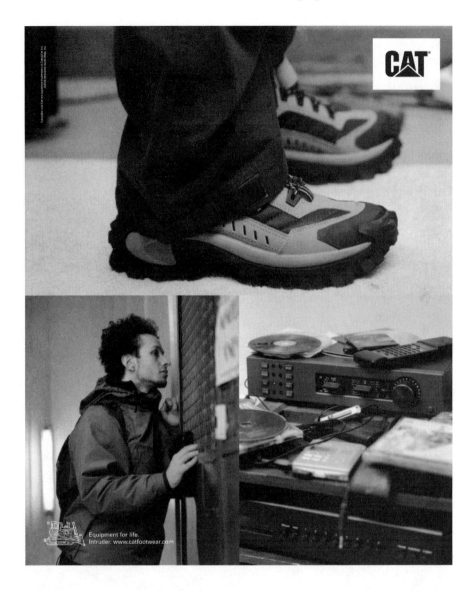

Figure 1.2   *Footwear Catalog*

Courtesy Caterpillar Inc.

Figure 1.3   *Footwear Catalog*

Courtesy Caterpillar Inc.

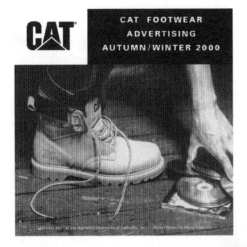

Figure 1.4   *Advertising Program Autumn/Winter 2000*

Courtesy Caterpillar Inc.

Can a single company brand appeal to many different cultures, or do different global regions call for different branding messages? Thanks to the Internet, television, and the growth in world travel for both business and pleasure, tastes and styles are becoming more similar from country to country. The brand appeal that works well in one locale is likely to also work well in others. This offers distinct advantages in product awareness when customers cross borders.

Corporations with firmly established domestic brands often find it relatively easy to transplant the brand to other cultures. Take Coca-Cola or Levi's: their ingredients and images are the same everywhere.

In its globalization effort, Coca-Cola made an important shift in its worldview by eliminating the concept of a "domestic" and "international" beverage business in the administrative structure of its worldwide operations. The corporation redefined its United States business as just one of six regional business units around the globe, believing that the labels "domestic" and "international" no longer apply in a global order. More and more companies are showing their global tendencies by abandoning organizational structures based on economic regions and are restructuring along global product lines.

Consumer product companies such as Coca-Cola, Levi's, and McDonald's have standardized production and distribution but still may customize their products to local tastes. The Coca-Cola corporate brand, epitomized so well by the special love affair between customer and product, is basically a simple concept. People around the world know Coke as a clean, refreshing beverage, which forestalls any need for the company to create a new global brand—this despite negative publicity resulting from recent contamination scares in three European countries (see Chapter 10).

McDonald's expansion outside the United States also developed rapidly, once the push to go truly global was established. Of the 1,750 McDonald's restaurants opened in 1999, for example, 90 percent were outside the U.S. in such major markets as Germany, France, England, Japan, Australia, and Brazil. The ubiquitous Golden Arches—already boasting more than 25,000 outlets and perhaps the most recognizable commercial symbol in the world—can be found, at this writing, in 116 countries.

The successful global branding of such companies as Coca-Cola and McDonald's bears heavily on the emergence of a global consumer whose tastes are increasingly attracted to global products and services. Teenagers in at least 83 countries, for example, are exposed increasingly to MTV and its many advertising messages. Teenagers in France probably have more in common with their counterparts in America than they do with their own parents. William Roedy, director of MTV Europe, remarks that teenagers in Europe "buy the same products, go to the same movies, listen to the same music, sip the same colas."

But such straightforward examples of global branding as McDonald's and Coca-Cola are not always the case. Corporate focus on building both a global company and a global brand sometimes produces conflicting results that can affect every aspect of the communications process.

Growing the Global Brand

The keys to growing a global brand are planning, setting targets and standards, and paying attention to detail. Companies with successful brand strategies do not leave brand building to chance, nor do they rely only on identity standards and brand policies. Rather, they support the brand with a core set of practices, generally including:

- Brand identity standards
- Brand management strategy
- A formal process for managing the brand
- A brand promise
- Widespread ability to articulate the brand promise
- A system to measure brand equity
- A performance review system linked to the brand

The problem global-minded CEOs face, however, is that to be responsive and efficient in a global economy, a corporation should decentralize responsibility for its lines of business, encouraging local partners and taking full advantage of their experience. Decision-making and accountability should be pushed downward to regional, if not local, product or marketing management.

However, in order to grow in today's marketplace, global or otherwise, a company needs a powerful, well-communicated brand. To protect the value of its brand, the company must maintain central control and consistency in its use and presentation. As might be expected, different companies use different approaches to resolve this apparent dichotomy and to select the best course in growing their global brand.

A research report published by The Conference Board points out that Levi Strauss relies on input from its staff in regional markets to help define key issues and avoid marketing traps. Robert Holloway of Levi Strauss explains: "One of the reasons we rely so heavily on our local people is that we know there are different cultural, developmental, economic, and even legal issues in each market. There is greater audience sophistication in some regions, while in others we might focus on building brand awareness."[8]

Microsoft's approach, described in the same study, is to have consistent themes worldwide when it comes to execution, but to localize some of the advertising. The degree of localization depends on the market. In English-speaking markets outside the United States, the ads are usually very similar. They are a little different in Europe and sometimes very different in Asia. "We do a good job designing our ads up front with these differences in mind," Ann Redmond explains. "We are a global brand and some level of continuity is very important to us."[9]

General Electric believes that its brand is perceived differently in different global regions: the tiered approach the company is taking in Asia is working well, James Harman of GE notes. "We assess where we are perceptually with our audience and then decide on how to support the brand. In some markets we may be able to start at point A and then leap to C. In others we may need to stay at point A for a long time. The trick is knowing when to move to the next tier."[10]

In a corporate culture we understand brand stewardship not so much as an issue of decentralization versus centralization, but as a commitment to establishing a common brand-based language throughout an entire organization. This means the integration of marketing, communications, and design. It also means the entire company, from finance to legal, makes decisions based on a brand-first mind-set.

Because the brand is generally recognized as a company's most valuable asset, the corporate role, therefore, is to actively encourage integration and consistency in how the brand is communicated. This ensures that consistency of expression is grounded in the core values and promise of the brand.

Even when a company has had long experience with corporate branding, fine-tuning may still be required in order to establish the global brand, or even a totally different approach, especially in developing markets.

The Communications Challenge

The quest for both global presence and a global brand poses a number of communications challenges to the corporation. Not the least of these is the need to address vigorously both governmental and financial communities, translating both corporate direction and vision culturally as well as literally. As increasingly changeable and culturally diverse audiences see and hear more, the communication of a clear, consistent message becomes more and more critical. Out of sight is indeed out of mind when it comes to branding. How businesses fare in globalization and global brand development depends to a great degree on how well they execute their communications. In this regard, there are four key areas on which companies should focus:

1. **Consistency of presentation.** The corporate brand and the way the company is presented through the elements of strategy, style, tone, logo, identity, and name integrity in all communications should be consistent around the world.

2. **Internal communications.** Communications strategies and messages should be sent to employees throughout all levels of the organization because your own people are the most credible and cost-effective disseminators of the corporate voice.

3. **Market support.** A company should provide communications support for all local market and product needs in terms of business strategy, organization, and skilled communications specialists.

4. **Efficiency.** As all companies want to get the most for their communications dollar, they must communicate efficiently by carefully targeting audiences, managing outside resources, planning budgets and controls, and cultivating the skills of all communications personnel.

Stewardship of the Brand

In the final analysis, there can be only one person responsible for global brand management. However the company is organized, it's almost always the chief executive officer who gives impetus for globalization, and it's the CEO who must be steward of the brand—global as well as domestic.

This only makes sense. It is the CEO who delineates the vision, shapes the company's presence in the global marketplace, and drives global growth. The ability to focus on the future is crucial to achieving success in the global village.

Business leadership qualities are especially demanding in a global market. The effective global leader is certainly someone who can handle more complexity and uncertainty than today's domestic managers are typically accustomed to—someone who relates well with different peoples and different cultures. He or she is a good listener, has an adventurous spirit, and believes there is more than one way to solve a business problem.

It takes time to build effective relationships with colleagues from around the world. They will undoubtedly have different approaches to business. Before a global team can run smoothly, everyone has to learn how well others in the group grasp the language and how they prefer to run meetings. Determine this at the start, or you may offend some people, leave others behind, and establish ground rules that few can live with.

Embarking on a major change calls for vision and commitment. When your vision is clearly stated and suffused throughout the organization, continue to focus on it. You need to get people to buy in. You need to hear what they conclude from what you say because, most likely, your decisions will be interpreted in many different ways. In other words, you and your managers need to elicit regular feedback.

Without a strong, focused will supported by active involvement, the CEO will have trouble handling the complexities of growth management. Problems are bound to occur if the CEO has difficulty expressing the company's mission; if he or she doesn't understand and/or can't articulate the company mission, who will?

Four Actions for the CEO

Many believe the future growth of the U.S. economy may well depend on ensuring free trade with our global neighbors. But according to Clark Johnson, chairman and CEO of Pier 1 Imports, this isn't likely to happen without active CEO support. He believes that for a company to achieve its fullest global potential, it has to recognize that growth rates throughout the world are greater than in the U.S. "To that end," he says, "CEOs need to be leading the charge."[11]

There are some specific actions a CEO can take to move such a mission along. For example, communicate with your company associates, including the employees, and point out the importance of free trade to their jobs, the company's progress, and its positive income growth. Encourage industry trade associates as well to join with other associations and support a national trade awareness campaign to counteract any negative spin from protectionists.

Also contact your congresspeople and senators personally in states where you have major corporate facilities and explain how exports influence the economic viability of your company. Another idea is to organize and implement a companywide letter-writing campaign to all other legislators.

It would seem pretty obvious that if the CEO cannot at least inspire his own employees about the benefits of free trade, he may find the legislators, media, and other influentials apathetic as well.

Involvement: How Much?

Research by The Conference Board finds that leaders who consider their companies globally successful spend 40 percent of their time on global issues, compared with an average of only 25 percent for all CEOs in the survey.[12]

In the early stages of globalization, experienced CEOs suggest that a viable presence is built from a foundation beginning with a discernible commitment of time, attention, and activity: time talking to visitors, employees, customers, and to other constituencies. In this way, you show your culture and you help your business. More than that, you learn all

IT'S ALL ABOUT THE PEOPLE

The global brand should always be in the forefront of a CEO's thoughts. This is distinctively and eloquently underscored by a message one CEO I know sent to his troops from his hospital bed in an intensive care unit. Ronald E. Ferguson, CEO of GeneralCologneRe Corporation, wrote the following:

> The metric for success and happiness here is very different. (I keep thinking about the comment I heard Mr. Buffett make—success is getting what you want, while happiness is wanting what you get.) The metric in ICU is not just about how Mr. Dow or how Mrs. Jones is doing—nor did I hear anybody mention anything about a combined underwriting ratio (in over eight days now!).
>
> The metrics here involve much more basic stuff about life and its fragility. In my case, after eight days in the Intensive Care Unit, the metric for success now seems to be reducing the number of tubes, leads, and catheters entering or leaving my body (started with seven—now down to only one).
>
> So I am heading in the right direction and expect a full recovery over the next month or so. In the process, I've learned a bunch of new things, some of which relate to our journey.
>
> I have watched and directly benefited from the services of another high-class team in action. This was the high-performing team of medical professionals in the ICU.
>
> The team and individual team members had deep and profound subject knowledge.
>
> They had an intense client focus—no confusion at all about why they were there.
>
> The team seemed to be largely self-directed.
>
> The team changed shape and composition as the client's needs changed.
>
> Technology was fully exploited by the team.
>
> There was—usually!—a sense of urgency.
>
> The individual team members seemed to truly respect/value each other and relied on one another's contributions.
>
> All in all, a high-performance group, and I was very fortunate to be on the receiving end. Let's make sure each of our clients feels the same way about our client teams. I have learned that more than ever, it's all about the people.

along the way. You see the numbers involved, but you also see some of the underlying issues that support the numbers. Unfortunately, the process can take up a lot of time.

The CEO's commitment expands to include company values, culture, focus and franchise. Says Robert Denham, CEO of Salomon Inc.: "Globalization allows a company to take advantage of a broad set of opportunities. But it should not be an excuse for loss of focus. The job of the global CEO is to protect and build a global franchise. It's only by building globally around a distinctive franchise that the company can create its own culture and its own identity. And without a distinctive culture and identity, a company can't hope to compete globally."[13]

Thus, in companies that are in the process of becoming global, the leadership role should focus on balancing global versus local identity in the eyes of employees, customers, government representatives, and other important constituencies.

Real Life in the Global Marketplace

As many companies are finding out, doing business globally is not simply taking a basic set of operations and applying them from one country to another. What might be appropriate in one locale might easily fail in another.

Global communication is a two-way street. The need to articulate company direction, values, and vision is always important, but the need to hear, understand, and respect the messages of other cultures is just as important. The attention paid to such communications can make or break the globalization effort. Companies that are serious about selling globally tend to understand this.

Well-communicated corporate branding can accomplish many ends. As pointed out, it can help launch a company, build its reputation, sell its products, and promote its stock. Global branding offers the same advantages. Corporation after corporation employs it now to ensure successful worldwide marketing, improve earnings, attract and motivate quality employees, and build company value—language barriers and cultural differences notwithstanding. It is not an easy assignment.

In short, don't underestimate the challenge of operating a global business enterprise. Communication in a multicultural world is a highly complex matter, requiring constant and careful attention. When a company is going through the major changes of globalization, it is especially important to communicate early and often, in greater detail and with a greater degree of frequency than might have been indicated before. This takes an enormous amount of energy, inventiveness, and patience.

As a result, many CEOs may have to change their perceptions as to what it takes to be a strong, dominant leader in the new global market-place. The leaders of tomorrow's global companies need to be innovative users of communications. For example, despite the obvious involvement of the CEO, some companies will expect their vice presidents, directors, and managers to communicate the global branding strategy down to their own people.

Naturally, some leaders may not be as articulate and persuasive communicators as others and will require special training, whenever practical. The skills of communication, however, are not the only lessons to be learned. With technology fast changing today's organization into one that is more complex, diverse, and decentralized, leaders should prepare themselves to succeed within the global village with its many new experiences and challenges.

The next chapter sets forth some basic steps to be taken by the CEO and appropriate members of company management in the global branding process. These guides are as much signposts as to why to pursue certain tactics as to what to do, when, and how.

Ten Key Points to Review and Remember

1. Globalization and corporate branding are the two prime forces in the way business is changing today.

2. Not only are companies focused on branding, but services, entertainment, media, and even people have become well-known brands.

3. Some global-minded companies, in an effort to increase profitability, adopt the strategy of acquiring leading global and local brands.

4. One common dilemma is how to decentralize business decisions to meet the needs of the local marketplace while at the same

time ensuring that the corporate brand is promoted via a globally consistent message in all forms of communication.

5. The corporate brand is a most significant asset—on average impacting stock performance by as much as 5 percent.

6. Five important market trends:
- Rising economies of scale
- Exploitation of experience curves and knowledge transfers
- Capitalizing on geographic image spillover
- Search for new growth opportunities
- Consolidation and globalization of the retail trade

7. The best practices used when adapting a corporate brand to global use:
- Set of brand identity standards
- Brand management strategy
- Formal process for brand management
- Brand promise
- Ability to articulate brand promise
- System to measure brand equity
- Review system linked to brand

8. Key areas of brand communications on which companies should focus:
- Consistency of presentation
- Internal communications
- Use of brand communication to support marketplace activity
- Efficiency of the branding program in achieving its goals

9. The CEO must be the steward of the global brand. After all, it's the CEO who delineates the company vision, shapes company presence in the marketplace, and drives global growth.

10. Global communication is a two-way street. The need to hear and understand the messages of other cultures is as important as articulating your own company's values and vision.

2

Ten Keys, Seven Steps, and Other Guides

GLOBAL BRANDING, LIKE corporate branding, is the process of projecting a positive company reputation. You can't expect foreign markets to accept your product without question, consider entering joint ventures with your company, invest in your endeavors, or work for you unless you make your company known and respected.

A well-understood, -directed, and -managed brand can have a significant impact. With a little forethought and the right strategy, nearly every company can benefit from it. Among its many advantages, a well-built global brand can:

- Communicate company character and purpose
- Call to mind products and services
- Maintain profit margins
- Reduce price volatility
- Make for greater selling efficiency
- Impact favorably on return on investment (ROI)
- Help recruit and retain quality employees
- Make new product and/or partnering introductions easier

- Help a company weather crises more readily
- Slow share erosion

The scope of global branding, like that of corporate branding, comprises everything the company says and does. It's a composite of all forms of a company's communications: corporate advertising, product brand advertising, investor relations, employee communications, government and media relations, and much, much more. It includes all expressions of corporate identity, such as corporate name, logo, and nomenclature, and even corporate architecture and interior design, when intended to create a single, specific impression. But its message must be able to transcend all borders.

In other words, global branding is an intentional, marketing-oriented communications platform across all business units, media, audiences, and national borders. It is the complete corporate culture as reflected by the company's reputation and conveyed to all chosen target constituencies.

Those corporations pursuing a global brand management program must use a planning process that is consistent across markets and products so that the brand presentation looks and sounds the same in Austria or Australia, Chile or China.

There is no one particular branding process considered best. It must, however, be perfectly clear who is responsible for the brand and its strategy. Whatever process is chosen, brand identity or vision, brand equity goals and measures, and brand-building programs that will be used both in and outside the company must be thoroughly and carefully delineated.

Certain guidelines are suggested by scrutinizing various effective branding programs. For one thing, the branding process should be a thorough analysis of both competition and customers. Customer analysis, for example, should transcend simple quantitative market research data, but should surely include, among the intelligence gathered, a detailing of the values potential customers respect and need. Managers need to know and understand those particular brand associations that best appeal to their customers because it is sometimes less expensive for companies to create ads locally than to create them at headquarters and then adapt them for individual markets.

The branding process should avoid preoccupation with product characteristics, while taking care to build in communications programs to convey the brand's identity to employees and company partners. Finally, don't forget the need to measure current brand equity and establish meaningful goals for its future development. Managers won't be able to determine how well they succeed in building their brands unless they develop efficient global brand and brand communications measurements. (More about this in Chapter 3.)

However the brand planning process evolves, the need for sharp, skillful brand leadership is always paramount. Doing "a good job" simply isn't enough, especially in the fast-expanding global marketplace. The steward of the brand—CEO, chief communications officer, brand manager, or whoever—must understand and have the power to implement a successful brand-building program. It goes without saying that he or she will require all assistance possible.

This chapter outlines ten keys and seven steps to create or re-create a strong, effective brand. They are not the only possible directions to take, but they represent a good place to start in constructing a company's branding program.

Ten Keys to a Strong Brand

Of the key attributes that can contribute toward a strong, successful brand, the following bear special consideration:

1. **Coherence.** Find the key promise. Think hard about what you're really selling to your customers. The answer is not always the product in the box. It may be the corporate brand promise on the box—that promise that tells customers why they should put faith in the company and its product.
2. **Consistency.** Take a long-term view. Branding, like R&D, is a long-term exercise and deserves thoughtful, long-term attention.
3. **Credibility.** Be true to your organization. A powerful brand can only be built on a credible foundation.
4. **Integration.** Align your organization. Support a consistent brand definition in each way you interact with your key audiences.
5. **Differentiation.** Stand out from the crowd. The companies that get noticed are the ones that stand for something unique.

6. **Risk.** Dare to be different. Successful leaders take calculated chances to follow their vision.
7. **Support.** Invest in the corporate brand. Continuity is critical. Reputation management is a slow and cumulative process. Be sure its funding is both adequate and ongoing.
8. **Focus.** Target your brand to critical audiences—internal as well as external. Be creative about using the right vehicles to deliver your message.
9. **Relevance.** Evolve with the changing times. Periodically reevaluate your brand, consider how others see you, and refine your strategies.
10. **Leadership.** Put someone in charge. Assign one point of accountability. Without a responsible branding leader, you cannot obtain full benefit from other keys.

(More about a special corporate branding officer in Chapter 12.)

Complex Challenges

The real difference between global and corporate branding is the complexity of the problems to be faced in the global marketplace. And these can be complex indeed. The crossing of borders with their differences in cultures, languages, religious traditions, and legal and political systems poses a special set of challenges, although guidelines for building a brand remain basically the same. (These challenges are covered in greater depth in Chapter 4.)

As primary steward of the brand, the CEO should be both multi-talented and multidimensional. In particular, he or she must be very comfortable in a global environment and able to deal effectively with world leaders as well as with people at all levels and in all corners of the world.

CEOs must learn how to cross traditional borders not merely to gain access to trading partners and the critical information they hold, but, equally important, to learn about "best practices" in the local marketplace. Traveling to different markets, the CEO will energize local teams and observe these "best practices" in action. The vision the CEO establishes for the organization and industry should always include such commitments.

BRANDING INVESTMENT IS LEADERSHIP OPPORTUNITY

Sir Adrian Cadbury, former chairman of Cadbury Schweppes, is very clear that a company intent on a world-class future does not make an investment in separate brands. Instead, its total investment in branding is a leadership opportunity to connect what the company stands for emotionally and strategically to those branded tracks it makes into particular markets and product positionings.

In an interview Sir Adrian stated that now that the concept of brand architecture has advanced to its present-day significance, whichever line you might consider Cadbury's most famous branded offer in the stores is really only a sub-brand to the Cadbury company brand and all that organization stands for.

> Heads of companies should set down what they feel their companies stand for. The character of a company is important to everyone in it and to those with whom the company does business. Belonging to a consistent company is important in earning a living in today's and tomorrow's competitive markets. Profitable growth and advance of the company reputation are the two measurements for judging success over time.
>
> A century-old Cadbury message reads: "Our policy in the future as in the past will be: first, the best possible quality—nothing is too good for the public." You could say that the character of the company depends on this kind of responsibility being acted on as the personal commitment of every individual and unit throughout the Cadbury Schweppes business.
>
> Change is constant—in markets, in ideas, in people, and in technology. . . . Objectives need to be built from the bottom up, but set from the top down.[1]

When it comes to building the global brand, certain leaders have a better track record than others. These men and women have mastered successful leadership communication skills and know how to inspire, orchestrate, and lead people. In turn, their followers reach new levels of satisfaction and productivity, achieve established objectives, and build winning organizations.

Leaders of this caliber are able to articulate a vision coherently in the context of strategic goals and corporate culture. They think strategically, paying attention to organizational strengths, yet remain receptive to new ideas. Successful brands can often be traced to such individuals.

The leader may determine the tone for the company reputation, but to ensure its proper guardianship, he should see that everyone in the organization shares a united view of the brand. The proposition for any successful brand needs to be utterly compelling. The customer should want to go "the extra mile" just to obtain it. But that is just the outer skin of the brand. Hopefully, the entire brand concept can be encapsulated in a simple vision so that the essence of the brand can be easily communicated and understood by all.

Seven Steps to a Global Brand

There are several principles to consider in order to achieve a successful global brand, and each authority will have his or her own preferred set of guidelines. Having discussed this extensively with various CEOs and corporate communications executives, I have come up with a set of seven pivotal steps to global branding. These may not be the only steps to follow, but they represent a good place to start.

1. Research Corporate Constituencies

Begin with research. Always begin with research. Study carefully those audiences—internal as well as external, foreign as well as domestic—that are important to your company. What is their knowledge of your company and its products and/or services? What is their opinion of your reputation? Find out and set benchmarks for future measurement. You'll want to know how you measure up in years to come.

Also develop input from key constituencies in various geographical markets. This will go a long way toward creating a viable across-boundaries understanding of critical marketplace similarities and differences—information indispensable to building a useful global brand.

Remember, you have many possible constituencies to focus on, some more appropriate than others. The list includes customers, prospects, employees, prospective employees (more important than ever in today's competitive global economy), investors, vendors, the trade, financial analysts, the media, opinion shapers, and government regulators (especially vital to globalization). And all these groups can be multiplied by the number of nations and cultures involved in your global expansion.

Therefore, for the first step in building your global brand, research is clearly indicated. It tells you where you are and in which direction you should be heading, and it establishes standards for future comparison. Research sets the tone for the steps to follow.

2. Understand Your Business

The second step is the completion of a thorough business analysis. You should understand your business fully, as well as its prospective place in the global market. This means setting guidelines and goals—especially for your communications programs—that are based on an in-depth understanding of your global objectives and recognition of the strategic benefits of corporate branding.

Too often full awareness of a brand's true value resides only at the highest levels of the organization. Establishing an appreciation of this value throughout the corporation, and developing methods for bringing presentation of the brand under control, can be a struggle. It requires achieving a mastery of brand management across numerous geographies, markets, and audiences.

It's important to treat brand building as a process that calls for discipline and long-term commitment. I believe the most powerful and successful corporate brands grow out of superior strategies, driven by superior insights, emerging from superior intelligence. Intelligence, especially, is central to "who we are" and "what we do." It provides the understanding, discernment, and inspiration needed to build a brand strategy that will resonate with all constituencies.

A particularly useful intelligence-gathering tool known as Core-Brand Analysis was developed by Corporate Branding, LLC with this end in mind. Used effectively by a number of leading corporations, this powerful proprietary program provides insight into the relationship between the investment in communications and the development of brand power. It demonstrates how generating this power can exert direct positive leverage on a company's stock price performance.

While advertising's impact on sales and earnings has long been understood and proven, the ability of a strong corporate—or global—

brand to have a positive impact on stock price has been intuitive at best. Until CoreBrand Analysis. (This relationship is covered in greater depth in Chapter 3.)

3. Advance the Vision

Decide on the reputation desired and create the strategy to support it. Then shape a strategic positioning document that distills the central purpose of your company. This document should be a single-minded proposition supported by well-researched facts, and it should differentiate your company from the competition in a positive manner. It should spring from your corporate reputation strategy, reflect financial and performance goals, and build on your competitive strengths.

Above all, reputation strategy should be infused with the company vision. This vision would already have been established, of course, most likely by the CEO. In broad, clear terms the document describes the business, its customers, products, investment, research and development, and growth and acquisition strategies. Now the vision must be evaluated and applied to the company's global future, as should the brand equity already available in company reputation.

Take special note that much depends on the thoroughness and integrity of your positioning document for it will be the source of future growth for the global brand.

4. Release the Power of Communications

With the branding groundwork laid, you then create a communications platform that validates the direction chosen and is targeted at key audiences through all the channels the company commands. Your platform defines and supports the power of your corporate brand. It declares who you are, what makes your company unique, and what your brand promises.

It is important, therefore, to harness the energy and integrate the various skills of your company's communications apparatus.

Communications must be viewed in the widest possible context. Sales communications, for example, should integrate the global messages into all communications, including direct sales, telemarketing, E-commerce, and so on. Marketing communications should take into account product advertising, direct mail, collateral materials, trade shows, etc.

Corporate communications include both public and investor relations, corporate advertising, websites, and, of course, company identity elements. For instance, "Coke red" is widely recognized around the world, and now Pepsi hopes that its blue packaging will become equally familiar.

Responsibilities throughout the organization must be assigned accordingly so that all aspects of the communications infrastructure work together to promote the brand. A word of caution: be sure to fund your branding program fully. Branding is too important a tool to risk wasting it because of insufficient communications dollars.

5. Set Up Your Communications Infrastructure

The prerequisite to effective global branding is a fully integrated communications infrastructure in place throughout all departments and business units and across all borders. Assemble your advertising and public relations professionals, investor relations experts, and human resource specialists into a global brand communications council. Working as a team, they should create and implement a branding communications program that can imprint your reputation on each of the identified audience groups.

Make sure your team bases its efforts on the carefully thought out communications platform so that all your company communications spring from a common corporate vision and are driven by the same business objectives and strategies.

The more decentralized the company is, the more organized its communications must become, and because of the wide variety of cultures and languages involved, this holds especially true in globalization. Company employees, on all levels and in all locales, should be thoroughly indoctrinated in the new global brand and committed to it. Everyone, from the CEO to the building custodian, should be able to describe in a couple of sentences what your company does and what its vision is.

Despite the volume of internal communications issued in companies today—so-called top-down communications, bottom-up messages, peer-to-peer communications, and the use of intranets—employees are not a captive audience. They have to be convinced through solid reasoning, training, and incentives that the real payoff of the branding program will be reflected ultimately in their paychecks.

The first step in global branding, as noted previously, states that a large number of audience groups must be approached. Needless to say, not even the most liberal communications budget can reach them all with equal effectiveness. The cost of advertising, promotion, and public relations is simply too high. Therefore, communications techniques should be selected for their appropriateness and efficiency, and should target audiences chosen with imagination and limited to those that seem to offer the greatest opportunities for corporate growth and profit.

6. Include Employees in the Message Mix

Communication to all groups must be clear, consistent, and appropriate to the target culture. And don't forget your employee audience. Their full and cooperative support can go a long way toward strengthening your company's image during any potential crisis. It's an important step to take in protecting your company's reputation and minimizing any possible damage should trouble occur.

For example, Coca-Cola's employees have long been indoctrinated in their corporate brand, and this well-established brand image throughout the world, supported so well by Coke's employees, has contributed much to offset the negative publicity generated by recent contamination scares in parts of Europe. (More on this in Chapter 10.)

The current excitement over massive recalls of Bridgestone/Firestone tires focuses not only on the tire company but on Ford as well, which has used Firestones on Explorers, Excursions, and some pickups. More than 100 deaths and over 400 serious injuries are linked to the tires because of alleged defects that cause the tires to lose their tread. The National Highway Traffic Safety Administration has opened an investigation, and in Venezuela, too, an investigation is under way because of local deaths allegedly linked to Ford Explorers equipped with Firestone tires.

At this writing it remains to be seen how these two companies, both with durable and substantive brand reputations, will weather the storm. One thing is sure, however: their solid reputations, long sustained and furthered by their employees, can only be of help.

In communicating the corporate/global brand, discordant, contradictory messages confuse and alienate audiences. Tersely asking all elements in the company to "increase the signal" of a particular message, however, is counterproductive, too. Rather than emphasize one repeatedly struck chord—the corporate message as mantra—the very nature of branding calls for a harmonious blend of communications.

It's about playing variations on a central theme that all the players truly understand and appreciate. Repetitive messages bore. Messages working together resonate in a way that is more powerful, more dimensional, more memorable to the audience.

As necessary as advertising and public relations are to a successful branding program, they are not the only powerful communications tools a company has at its disposal. Unique among all elements of corporate or global branding is the work force itself. Employees are not only an important target audience, they are a channel of communication, and, in reality, part of the company message itself. Employees can make or break the brand.

The 3M company, for example, utilizes many ways of communicating to its employees. Councils, conferences, committees, and management groups of many kinds are employed. The word comes down through all these mechanisms, as well as through the usual media of magazines, newspapers, E-mails, and so forth. Of particular interest, there is a 3M TV system, a global network of television hookups that can be set up in many of the company's locations around the world and can broadcast live or taped messages to all employees.

7. Measure the Performance

These steps started with research—benchmarking your corporate reputation with your various audiences. The final step in the process takes us back to research: measuring to track progress toward goals and to determine the effectiveness of branding communications. Performance measurement involves analytical and market research that identifies reputation elements and compares results with established benchmarks to provide management with evidence that goals have been achieved. (See Chapter 3 for an analytical perspective on the drivers of return on investment of corporate brand communications.)

Many companies set up tracking systems in the marketplace in order to make important operational decisions using the measurements. Such a program takes time, but it's the step that completes the branding circle for the experienced marketer. For example, Jonathon Gould, senior vice president at MasterCard, says that to measure the results of their branding program, they conduct global tracking studies, in addition to managing against strong market share growth targets.

Focusing on two or three different key audience groups including employees, customers, and investors, ITT Industries did both pre- and postactivity measurements for an advertising/identity program launch. Although general findings were mixed, the employee survey results were strong and suggested that employees both understood the company better and felt more positively toward it after the launch of the program. Pretesting that group the summer before the launch and then post-testing the following spring, the company saw some very positive trends.

ITT Industries customer group was more difficult to measure because it is so diverse, including just about everything from mining to pulp and paper processing to chemical production to defense contracting. There are four major management companies, and each has a different customer base. And even within each of those, there are many customer segments.

The investor community, too, presented a mixed picture. There was, however, a strong relationship between the awareness of ITT Industries advertising and familiarity with the company. Those with greater familiarity viewed the company more favorably.

Properly followed, the foregoing steps should lead to a branding program with a number of important characteristics. Key attributes, shared by a number of the world's strongest brands, include:

- The brand delivers the benefits customers look for.
- The brand is both relevant and consistent.
- The brand employs a full range of communication and marketing activities to build equity.
- Brand managers fully understand what the brand means to each constituency.
- The brand is properly supported for the long haul.
- Brand equity is monitored on a continuing basis.

CREATING GLOBAL BRAND POWER[2]

We have examined some of the key steps needed to build and communicate a new, powerful, worldwide brand, and a number of traits it should demonstrate. Now let's see how one particular company, ITT Industries, has used some of these ideas in its own global branding process.

Two years after having been spun off from ITT Corporation, ITT Industries conducted research on awareness of the company and its brand among key stakeholder audiences. Did people recognize the name, know what it stands for, know the products it offers? Did they understand the core strengths and weaknesses of the company and its divisions?

Results of the study were disquieting. "ITT" was recognized and associated with quality products, but ITT Industries was a different matter. Hotels, casinos, and telephone equipment were listed as the company's main businesses by two-thirds of the respondents. The people were obviously confused. They were thinking of the other ITT—ITT Corporation. No wonder. That other ITT had been getting all the publicity for years and had its name on all kinds of products and services.

"It was apparent that branding and corporate identity was one of our major challenges," says Thomas Martin of ITT Industries. "People knew the name. They just had no idea what it meant. Was it hotels, was it insurance, was it manufacturing—what was it? It's really been sort of a brand confusion that we've tried to clear up."

The confusion prevailed despite the fact that ITT Industries had recently acquired the largest pump producer in the world, Goulds Pumps, with much press coverage. Furthermore, the company already had such other well-known and highly regarded brand names as Flygt, Cannon, and KONI in its stable.

"The other big issue," Martin adds, "is that we've got about 35 product brand lines in the company. What we've tried to do is build a system that would, on a global basis, link the corporate brand to all

continued

of our various product areas, which of course have many different looks, many different markets, and many different customer bases. We have tried to make our corporate brand program very flexible in order to accommodate them."

An End to Confusion

The study indicated that the substantive businesses of ITT Industries remained a mystery to many of the people it needed to reach and influence. There was an obvious need for a corporate branding program that could effectively distinguish ITT Industries from any other ITT, anywhere in the world. The company had to bring together its many successful businesses under one powerful global brand and put an end to any confusion among prospective customers, investors, employees, and other target audiences.

Thomas Martin: "We have good people, we make good products, we achieve good financial results, we are a good environmental and corporate citizen, but we weren't getting credit for that in the way we should have been. Our original corporate identity, which was established when we became an independent company, had always been intended as temporary. Instinctively, we all knew that we needed a more distinct and memorable logo. As employees, we often were put in the situation of explaining who we worked for, only to have to re-explain it a short time later."

A New Identity

Martin assembled a branding team that included corporate identity consultant Landor Associates, corporate advertising agency Doremus, and public relations firm Ketchum. They started work on a corporate identity initiative that would tell the ITT Industries story to the outside world through a program of advertising and public relations, plus a new visual identifier.

From the start, there was the option of abandoning the ITT name altogether, with its associated confusion. Martin says this was considered, but not for long because it would not have been cost effective: it's expensive to establish a new name in the marketplace.

But the ITT name had a reputation as an engineering company, and so Martin and others believed they could refocus people on the things that had made the company special in the past.

The company's new identity incorporates three elements: the ITT Industries name, the "engineered blocks" core symbol, and the "engineered for life" tag line.

The symbol grows out of the ITT letters, presenting them as equally proportioned, interlocking pieces that unite to form a solid whole. "It speaks to the whole interwoven aspect of the company, and speaks to the engineering precision that we employ in all of our various markets," Martin says. "It connotes precision, strength, unity, and underscores the company's engineering heritage. The tag line was a real breakthrough because it immediately crystallized everything the company was trying to communicate."

"We wanted to convey durability and reliability because everything we make has to have those qualities. The pump we supply for the bottom of the well has to work every day, in all kinds of conditions. The night vision equipment we manufacture can't fail in a critical situation. Almost all of the products we make are 'mission critical'"

ITT Industries launched its corporate advertising and identity program around the world. The company derives about half of its revenues from outside the U.S., and operates facilities in more than fifty countries. The ad campaign utilized both television and print and presented the message that the products ITT Industries makes are vital to the economies of the world—mission-critical products that have to work every time they are called upon.

The combination of TV and print made a powerful impression. Television advertising generated immediate awareness of ITT as a global, world-class company. It reached almost 70 percent of the company's key stakeholders, including investors, customers, prospects, and other business decision makers. The print ads, meanwhile, offered a more detailed look at the company and its products, highlighting issues such as growth potential.

continued

A Meeting in a Box

A communications council, consisting of marketing and public relations people from the company's various business units, orchestrated the rollout of the new identity, using what Martin describes as "a meeting in a box" turnkey kit. The team also monitored the best use of the new logo using a guidelines manual.

Some of the individual ITT Industries brands might not be as prominent now as they were before, but according to Martin, the new identity has been well received. While the program originated due to the support of the CEO, it has now gained support from the people in all of the operating companies. But Martin believes results must continue to prove to line management that the identity effort and the corporate advertising can pay for itself.

He adds: "It's my belief that in an uncertain world, customers want to get a sense that the company they are doing business with is going to be around for a while. For current employees, a campaign like this can do a lot to raise the level of pride they feel in the company. And prospective employees, with more than 3,000 companies listed on the New York Stock Exchange, will be more likely to take us seriously. It doesn't hurt to do something that makes us stand out in the minds of our investors.

"A campaign like this pays off in a lot of ways."

Building a successful brand can sometimes be tremendously difficult. When a company focuses on improving one brand characteristic, other attributes often suffer. The trick is to determine how a brand embodies all desired attributes and then evaluate any future move from all possible perspectives. For example, how will a new ad campaign affect the brand's perception by customers? Will a simple tweak in positioning offset any potential damage caused if customers feel the company has been inconsistent in its messages? And so forth.

The power of a brand actually can be found in the minds of customers, in what they have learned about the brand over time. Thus consumer knowledge is really the core of brand equity. Dollars spent each year on marketing are not so much expenses but investments in what customers know, remember, perceive, and believe about the brand, all of which can influence future directions for the brand to take.

Building a Brand Platform

When Ciba Specialty Chemicals, Inc., was spun off from Novartis International AG it formed a new company dedicated to creating and selling specialty chemicals for business-to-business customers. Symbolizing the company's transformation and new-found independence, Ciba Specialty Chemicals introduced a six-color butterfly as its new corporate logo, along with the tag line "Value Beyond Chemistry."

Ciba, however, lacked a central brand strategy for managing its corporate and product brands over the long term, and Corporate Branding LLC was given the task to help turn the logo into a brand by giving it meaning, creating ways to put it to work, and devising processes to protect it as a business asset.

A strategy was created for the Ciba brand based on qualitative and quantitative research with customers, internal business leaders, and external opinion leaders. The strategy evolved around three major points:

- A platform that defines the core of the Ciba brand
- A product-naming strategy that links the company's products to the corporate brand
- An application strategy for allowing the Ciba corporate brand to show through on select customers' products as an ingredient

Patrick Gorman, global head of advertising and branding for Ciba Specialty Chemicals, elaborated in an interview with the author on how his company entered into a branding program designed to leverage the power of both its corporate brand and individual product brands, in a variety of ways.

The first thing we did, of course, was some benchmark research on how Ciba was perceived by financial communities, customer communities, media, and other constituencies. Our suspicions were correct: there was a lot of equity, a lot of positive associations, with the name. Thus it made sense to go ahead with our branding strategy, to leverage the power of the corporate name through master branding of product names. Products that had been called Tinosorb are now called Ciba Tinosorb. We are also trying to raise the profile of the brand among all audiences with advertising.

The most interesting strategy we had was using the brand as a marketing tool to go out to our indirect customers. Rather than just promoting our products and capabilities to our direct customers—who were often one, two, or three links removed from the actual user of a product—we were trying to increase the awareness of Ciba's capabilities amongst the end users, or the links in between the end user and our direct customer. This sort of branding can cement client relationships, create a pull-through demand for the product, and generate licensing revenue.

I should point out that we are at the beginning of implementing a branding strategy. The research we did and the work we did with Corporate Branding helped us identify a brand platform for the company, including a core promise, attributes, and personality characteristics. Corporate Branding worked with the branding folks here and our senior management in identifying each of these.

Personality characteristics were identified as Ciba being an agile, insightful, aggressive, and ethical company. Our attributes were innovation, transformation, and reliability. And the core promise is that we supply inspiring effects.

Effects are things like color, strength, and performance. Ciba's direct customers incorporate these and their benefits into a wide range of products. We say "inspiring" because it's really not just what we make, but what we make possible. In other words, rather than just being a chemical company that is focused on test tubes and molecules, we have insight into the real world and we look for needs and problems. And where we find them, we try to work with partners to create solutions.

As an example, Gorman cited skin cancer, now the most common form of cancer in the world. About 90 percent of the incidences of skin cancer are a result of exposure to the sun's ultraviolet radiation. Though most people know they can reduce the risk of damage to exposed skin by applying a good sunscreen, they don't realize that UV radiation can penetrate their clothes and thus also cause damage to unexposed skin.

Ciba, which makes ingredients that go into sunscreens and into plastics, so they don't degrade in the sun, is working with its garment manufacturing partners on making clothing more protective against the sun's ultraviolet radiation. You can now buy clothes that have UV protection

Value beyond chemistry

Figure 2.1 *Logo*

Courtesy Ciba Specialty Chemicals Inc.

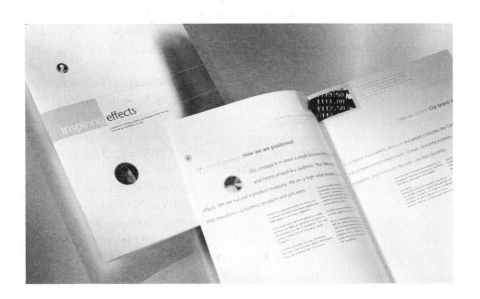

Figure 2.2 *Strategy Program*

Courtesy Ciba Specialty Chemicals Inc.

Figure 2.3   *Product Hangtag*

Courtesy Ciba Specialty Chemicals Inc.

from Ciba built into the fabric. These are labeled "UV protection by Ciba," which helps the garment manufacturer to differentiate its products from competition, and Ciba to increase its visibility. And you can also get detergent and rinses that will add UV protection with each wash.

One of the key benefits of Ciba's branding strategy is that it helps shift the company from a product-focused to a more market-focused company. And, as you can see, Ciba leverages the power of its brand beyond direct customers, sometimes all the way to end customers, in order to create valuable new business opportunities for all of its stakeholders—investors and employees as well its customers.

The essence of the corporate brand is the promise; the promise articulates the emotional heart of the brand. The key to the brand promise

Figure 2.4   *Identity Guidelines*

Courtesy Ciba Specialty Chemicals Inc.

is not about what a company makes; it should be about what it makes possible. No matter how carefully a company may follow "magic" steps, keys, or guidelines, the creation and maintenance of a strong global brand is never easy. Sometimes there can be just too many obstacles to overcome. This book covers a number of these challenges—differences in cultures, languages, values, political systems, for example—in Chapter 4.

Ten Key Points to Review and Remember

1. You can't expect foreign markets to accept your product without questions, consider entering joint ventures with your company, invest in your endeavors, or work for you unless you make your company known and respected.

2. Global branding, like corporate branding, is an intentional, marketing-oriented communications platform across all business units, media, audiences, and national borders.

3. Among many other advantages, a well-built brand can:
   - Communicate company character and purpose
   - Call to mind products and services
   - Help recruit and retain quality employees
   - Make partnering introductions easier
   - Influence stock price and ROI

4. Ten special keys to a strong brand:
   - Coherence
   - Consistency
   - Credibility
   - Integration
   - Differentiation
   - Risk
   - Support
   - Focus
   - Relevance
   - Leadership

5. The CEO must be both multitalented and multidimensional, able to function creatively and effectively in a world of diverse cultures and traditions, complex economic challenges, and fierce competition.

6. Seven steps to a global brand:
   - Research corporate constituencies
   - Understand your business
   - Advance the vision
   - Release the power
   - Set up communications infrastructure
   - Include employees in message mix
   - Measure the performance

7. A strong brand maximizes certain important characteristics:
   - Delivering benefits customers desire
   - Staying relevant and consistent

- Using a full range of communication and marketing activities to build equity
- Communicating a message understood by all audiences
- Giving and maintaining proper long-term support
- Continually monitoring brand equity

8. Creating a new identity may end brand confusion.

9. Building and effectively using brand equity is a continuous process.

10. Some companies use brand as a marketing tool to increase awareness among end users.

3

Bottom Line on Corporate Brand Investment

BILLIONS OF DOLLARS are spent each year by companies around the world attempting to improve their corporate images. These corporations recognize that being held in high esteem by customers, employees, stockholders, and the public at large is important to their long-term success.

Until recently these companies have been unable to put any reliable measure on the payback from these investments. The research done at Corporate Branding, LLC has changed this. During the past 10 years Corporate Branding has studied the relationships between corporate advertising, corporate brand image, sales growth, stock market multiples (e.g., price/earnings ratio), stock price, and shareholder value. A model of these effects is shown in Figure 3.1.

As the model illustrates, corporate communications directly impact corporate image. In addition to providing general information about product and service features, availability, price, etc., advertising helps build brand recognition and image, which in turn help develop preference and sales. Advertising can also help build familiarity with and enhance favorability toward the company providing these products and services. This can help decidedly in future marketing activities.

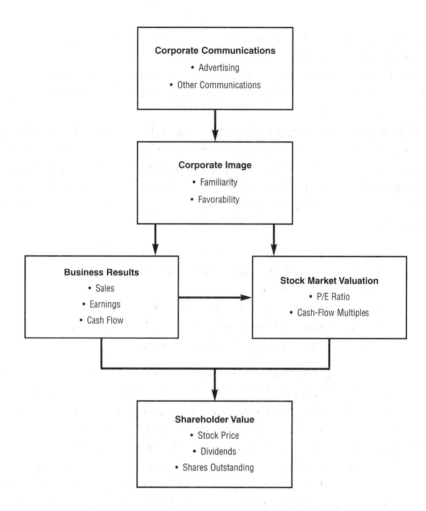

Figure 3.1   *Linkages Between Corporate Communications and Shareholder Value*

Three Favorability Measures

Corporate Branding, LLC views corporate image as the combination of how familiar the target audience is with the company and—among those sufficiently familiar—how favorable these people are toward the company. Three favorability measures are used: (1) overall reputation, (2) perception of management, and (3) investment potential.

Continuous surveys of business decision makers and financial influencers are conducted to measure familiarity and favorability among this target audience for 800 major corporations in the U.S. Many of these corporations are global in scope, and some have their headquarters overseas. Familiarity and favorability are combined for each company to produce a proprietary single measure of corporate image that we call *CoreBrand Power*.

Corporate Branding has found substantial evidence that improving a company's familiarity and favorability can significantly improve its stock price over time. This finding is a major breakthrough and answers the age-old marketing question: "What financial returns can I expect from my communications investment?" This dynamic occurs for two reasons:

1. When image improves, business results typically improve because sales tend to grow faster than with lower image, all other things being equal.
2. When image improves, the stock market tends to place a higher valuation on the company's stock through the price/earnings ratio and cash flow multiple.

Thus image improvement tends to improve both earnings and cash flow and the multiples the stock market places on those results. This, of course, results in a higher stock price than would otherwise occur with a weaker corporate image. In addition, the enhanced earnings and cash flow provide a basis to sustain or improve dividend payout.

Corporate Branding has been studying this potent relationship for several years. At first, the connection of advertising to stock price was examined, but no significant link was found. A breakthrough came when the effect was separated into two parts: (1) the link between advertising and corporate image, and (2) the link between corporate image and stock price. Corporate Branding recently completed an extensive reanalysis of these relationships after adding 1998 advertising, image, and financial data to the database.

Relating Corporate Communications to Corporate Image

The relationship between communications and image was analyzed using a base of 400 publicly traded corporations. These included industrial, consumer, transportation, financial, and utility companies across 60 industry classes. To be included, a company had to be tracked in the Value Line Investment Survey (a widely recognized premier source of U.S. financial data) and had to have Corporate Branding image data for at least the four years 1995 through 1998. Twenty-seven of the thirty Dow Jones industrial stocks are included. While the database focuses primarily on large companies, a number of medium and small companies are also included.

The advertising data were obtained from Competitive Media Reporting (CMR) and include only that portion of company advertising that specifically mentions the company name. Rome Report data were included to capture trade advertising. Both of these sources are widely understood to be the most comprehensive means to measure advertising investment. Any product or other advertising that did not include the company name was omitted.

Advertising spending is very disproportionate across this sample of 400 companies: 20 percent of the companies account for 88 percent of the corporate advertising spending while several spent nothing at all. The lowest 40 percent each spent less than $1 million per year, while the top 20 percent averaged more than $140 million per year.

Among the 400 companies studied, Coca-Cola stands out as having had the highest level of familiarity, favorability, and CoreBrand Power at the end of 1999. Walt Disney was second in familiarity, Microsoft second in favorability. The top five CoreBrand Power companies were Coca-Cola, Microsoft, Walt Disney, Campbell Soup, and Johnson & Johnson, in that order. The five database companies with the lowest level of CoreBrand Power were Premark International, Albany International, Pittway Corp., Acuson Corp., and Danka.

A Positive Association

Figure 3.2 shows the positive association that exists between CoreBrand Power and corporate advertising. The 40 percent of companies that averaged less than $1 million per year invested in corporate advertising have a CoreBrand Power score that averaged about 17 on a 100 point scale. The top 20 percent, which averaged over $140 million per year in corporate advertising spending, have a CoreBrand Power average score of over 50.

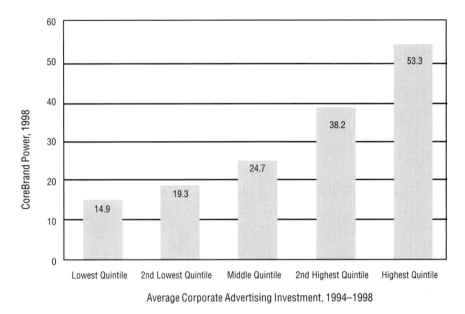

Based on 400 companies with 80 represented in each bar.

Figure 3.2   *CoreBrand Power vs. Corporate Advertising Investment*

This relationship, of course, does not prove that corporate image is caused by corporate advertising alone. Certainly there are other factors that contribute to a strong corporate image. The companies that spend a large amount on advertising tend to be large, well-known corporations. They usually have a large presence in the marketplace and a large market capitalization (stock price times the number of shares outstanding). A strong correlation exists between advertising, sales, market capitalization, and CoreBrand Power.

Casual relationships are best shown by examining changes over time. In an extensive analysis of CoreBrand Power, familiarity and favorability were examined separately. Average annual change in each from 1995 through 1998 was associated with the average annual corporate advertising investment from 1944 to 1998. The relationship between percentage point change in familiarity and advertising investment is shown in Figure 3.3.

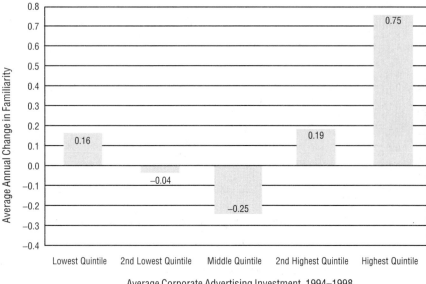

Based on 400 companies with 80 represented in each bar.

Figure 3.3   *Change in Familiarity vs. Corporate Advertising Investment*

The chart shows that heavy investment in advertising usually improves familiarity with the company. This is even more remarkable than it appears because it overcomes the tendency of "regression toward the mean." (In layman's terms, high familiarity companies tend to drop over time, low familiarity companies tend to grow over time, and average companies tend to stay average.) Empirical studies have shown, for example, that it is difficult for successful companies to maintain a high level of profitability, market share, familiarity, or CoreBrand Power. Conversely, very low levels tend to increase, often even in the absence of forces that normally tend to increase them.

Regression toward the mean is shown for familiarity in Figure 3.4, which plots percentage point change in corporate familiarity against the beginning (1995) level of familiarity.

As Figure 3.4 shows, the eighty companies that had the lowest level of familiarity in 1995 showed an average increase in familiarity of more than one percentage point per year over the next three years. The ones that started with high familiarity tended to lose position.

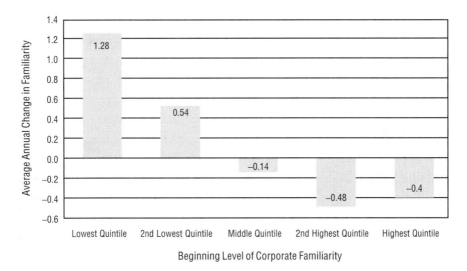

Figure 3.4 *Change in Familiarity vs. Beginning Level*

When change in familiarity is adjusted for regression toward the mean, the resulting pattern is very similar in shape to the pattern showing the amount spent on advertising. Corporate advertising spending is highly correlated with change in familiarity adjusted for regression to the mean.

Favorability Shows Similar Pattern

An analysis of favorability shows a very similar pattern to familiarity. Change in favorability shows a strong positive association with advertising investment, which becomes even stronger after adjustment for regression toward the mean. The top advertising group averaged twice the improvement in favorability as the second highest group after adjustment, while the bottom three groups averaged a decline in favorability.

Change in familiarity and change in favorability combine to produce results that show a similar pattern for CoreBrand Power. As Figure 3.5 illustrates, the highest spenders on average gain 2.2 percentage points of CoreBrand Power after adjusting for its beginning level. This

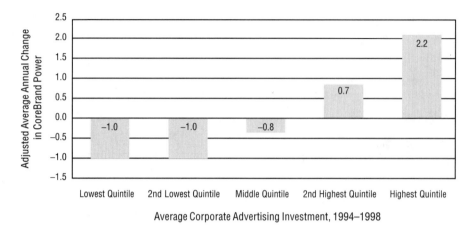

*Adjusted for beginning level of CoreBrand Power. Based on 400 companies with 80 represented in each bar.

Figure 3.5   *Adjusted Change in CoreBrand Power vs. Corporate Advertising Investment*

adjustment is usually downward because the beginning level is usually high. Stated another way, high CoreBrand Power corporations require higher levels of advertising than their lower CoreBrand Power counterparts just to maintain their level.

The level of advertising was found to have a much stronger effect on familiarity than on favorability. This is to be expected, of course, since advertising can more easily create overall awareness than persuade someone to "like" something.

Other factors in addition to the amount of corporate advertising and the beginning level were found to influence familiarity and favorability. After accounting for these two dominating effects statistically, CoreBrand Power tended to improve more among companies that had:

- A smaller base on their level of sales revenue
- Low stock market "betas," meaning less stock price volatility and less association with moves in the general stock market
- High expected future cash flow growth
- Shown a strong gain in stock price during the previous year
- Relatively more of their favorability based on their "investment potential" score

- Relatively less of their favorability based on their "overall reputation" score

Relating Corporate Image to Business Results

Drawing on this extensive analysis, Corporate Branding researchers hypothesized that companies that improve their corporate image would grow sales revenue faster than those that did not, all other things being equal. This increase in the rate of sales growth would result in improved earnings and cash flow over the longer term.

However, because so many different factors affect a company's sales, they expected to find only a modest contribution from corporate brand image and would not have been surprised if no statistically significant results were found. Some of these other effects that could outweigh the power of corporate image include mergers, acquisitions, spin-offs, new business development, new markets entered, old markets exited, aggressiveness in capacity expansion and marketing, and the inherent strength of the company's business.

A key reason for the belief that corporate image was a factor driving business success was based on prior empirical research conducted by the Strategic Planning Institute in Cambridge, Massachusetts. During the 1970s and 1980s a large-scale research effort was undertaken by the Strategic Planning Institute to understand elements related to business profitability. Several hundred companies participated in this research, called PIMS (Profit Impact of Market Strategy), and a database of more than 2,000 businesses was developed and made available for research. Each business was described by several hundred factors, one of which was relative product image/corporate reputation described on a five point scale. While not among the most important causes related to business profitability, reputation was nevertheless significantly associated with market share, product quality, and profit margin.

Growth in sales can be thought of as consisting of two distinct parts: (1) growth of the market or industry in which the company competes, and (2) growth in the share of those sales. A company often has little influence over the growth of industry sales because this frequently depends on the underlying demand for the type of product or service offered and on where the industry is positioned in its "life cycle."

Thus, companies frequently become involved in battles for market share. It is important therefore to understand the factors related to change in market share and, from Corporate Branding's perspective, whether market share change depends on corporate brand image.

This portion of Corporate Branding's analysis included 492 companies with sales and image data available from 1995 through 1998. Companies whose sales were greatly distorted by large mergers, acquisitions, or spin-offs were excluded. The companies studied were classified into 60 industries. The industry groupings were based on the Value Line Investment Survey classification, but in some cases similar industries were combined. For example, "Steel, General" was combined with "Steel, Integrated," and "Auto Parts, OEM" was combined with "Auto Parts, Replacement." Not all Value Line industry groups were represented in the database.

Sales revenue data were obtained from the Value Line Investment Survey. Sales in 1998 were compared to sales in 1995. For each of these two years, a share of industry sales was computed by dividing each company's sales by the sum of the sales of all companies in its industry. Some distortion will occur in doing this since it is impossible to define industries to include only companies that compete in identical product markets. Large diversified corporations usually have many varied businesses that compete in a variety of markets, and it is difficult in many cases to assign a company to a single industry.

Again, image was defined as CoreBrand Power. For each company, the 1995 value was used as the base value. A share of CoreBrand Power was calculated for each company by dividing the CoreBrand Power by the sum of the values of all the companies in the same industry.

A measure called CoreBrand Share Differential was computed for 1995 by subtracting the 1995 share of sales revenue from the Core-Brand Share. The key hypothesis was that share of sales (i.e., market share) would move toward CoreBrand Share over time. Thus we would expect that share of sales would increase when CoreBrand Share Differential was positive, and decrease when it was negative. Because of the many other factors affecting sales mentioned previously, many exceptions to this were expected.

Other researchers have found that market share is often influenced by share of voice: the proportion of advertising and other communications spent by each competitor in the market. The presence of this effect was tested using Competitive Media Research (CMR) data for advertising spending. Again, only spending that referenced the corporate name was included.

Three Central Questions

Three central questions were addressed in this research:

1. Does image as measured by CoreBrand Power have an effect on relative sales growth?
2. If so, does it vary by industry?
3. Is the effect stronger or weaker than the direct effect of advertising (i.e., share of voice)?

The research clearly demonstrated that CoreBrand Power does have a statistically significant relationship with relative sales growth, and that image is a strong second-level determinant of relative sales growth. This effect is shown in Figure 3.6, which plots the average percentage point change in share of sales vs. CoreBrand Share Differential. The 492 companies were divided into five groups with 98 or 99 in each group, based on their CoreBrand Share Differential—the difference between the 1995 CoreBrand Power share and the 1995 share of industry sales.

As can be seen, the companies where CoreBrand Power was lowest—compared to sales on average—lost about 1½ percentage points of market share in the three years from 1995 through 1998. The highest companies on average gained about one share point. Less difference occurred in the middle three groups.

Two tests were used to measure statistical significance. The first was to calculate the correlation coefficient between change in share of sales and CoreBrand Share Differential across the 492 companies. This resulting correlation coefficient was +0.33, which is highly significant—well above the 99 percent confidence level.

The second test was to determine for how many of the companies the share of sales moved toward the CoreBrand Share Differential and for how many it moved away. For 274 (55.7 percent) of the companies, the share of sales moved in the expected direction, i.e., toward the Core-Brand Share Differential. For 218 (44.3 percent) of the companies, it moved in the opposite direction. If image had no influence, 50 percent of the companies would be expected to move each way. There is only a

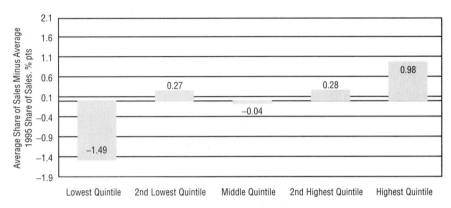

Figure 3.6   *Average Change in Share of Sales vs. CoreBrand Share Differential*

0.6 percent chance—less than one in a hundred—that the 274/218 split would have occurred by chance if there were no image effect. However, the fact that many companies moved counter to expectations shows that CoreBrand Power is a strong second-level factor rather than a primary driver of market share change.

In testing for the second research question, significant industry differences were expected to exist. In some industries, such as Soaps and Cosmetics, great differentiation exists and sales are more often based on image. In commodity product businesses, such as Metals, it might be expected that image would have a lesser role in driving change in share of sales.

Industry differences were tested by computing the correlation coefficient described previously among the companies in each of the 60 industries. While large differences did exist as expected, the high vs. low correlation industries did not neatly match expectations. The correlations were often distorted by one or two "outlier" companies, often a very large company whose share of sales greatly exceeded its share of CoreBrand Power. Further research is needed on this issue.

The third research question is related to whether share of voice (i.e., share of advertising dollars spent) had a stronger or weaker relationship with change in share of sales. Many advertising and marketing professionals recommend the use of share of voice as an indicator of future trends in market share.

This research indicated that share of voice was a slightly weaker factor than share of CoreBrand Power but still statistically significant in driving sales share change. The correlation coefficient between change in share of sales and 1995 share of voice minus 1995 share of sales was +0.28, which is slightly less than share of CoreBrand Power but still highly significant.

Share of sales moved toward share of voice for 267 companies. It moved away from share of voice for the other 225. The probability of this split, given no image effect, is about 3 percent. The effect of share of voice is strongest at very low levels of advertising (zero or near zero), where it tends to depress share of sales, and at very high levels of advertising, where it tends to improve share of sales.

In the multivariate analyses it was found that share of CoreBrand Power was the stronger effect and essentially drove out the share of voice effect. The correlation between the two was 0.67 across the 492 companies. We believe it is best to model these effects by relating image change to advertising spending, and relating market share change to image change.

Relating Corporate Image to Stock Market Valuation

Change in stock price can be thought about as consisting of two parts:

- Changes in sales, cash flow, earnings, dividends, and book value—the key measures of company performance
- Changes in the multiples, i.e., premiums the market grants to the company based on its past performance and expected future performance

Large variations always exist in these multiples. For example, the current (at this writing) P/E ratio for Microsoft is about 30, while that of General Motors is about 6.

This variation prompted two important questions in the minds of our researchers:

- Do price/earnings ratios and cash flow multiples (CFM) tend to move toward some "normal" expected long-term of P/E or CFM?
- Is this normal level affected by the CoreBrand Power of the company?

To answer these questions, researchers used the same sample of 400 companies employed to analyze the communications/image relationship. The analyses show that the answer to both questions is clearly yes. In these analyses it was found better to focus on the CFM than on P/E for four reasons:

- CFM is more stable with less year-to-year fluctuation.
- Cash flow is much less likely to be negative than earnings. (Negative numbers give nonsense ratios.)
- Cash flow is less subject to accounting differences than are earnings.
- The results explained more of the variance in CFM than in P/E.

The "normal" level of the CFM was obtained by analyzing the variation in the actual level. Many factors were found to be associated with the cash flow multiple, and as expected, most of them were financial.

The relationship between the 1998 cash flow multiple and CoreBrand Power at the beginning of 1998 is shown in Figure 3.7. A five-point difference exists between the 80 companies with the highest level of CoreBrand Power and the 80 with the lowest level.

Six other factors were found to be strongly related to the cash flow multiples. They tend to be higher when:

- Future expected cash flow growth is high.
- Earnings are a high percentage of cash flow.
- The company is strong financially.
- Earnings are more predictable.
- Stock price is more volatile, i.e., the "beta" is high.
- The investment potential portion of favorability is high relative to the management competence portion.

Several other significant but less important factors are also included in Corporate Branding's model for the normal cash flow multiple. In

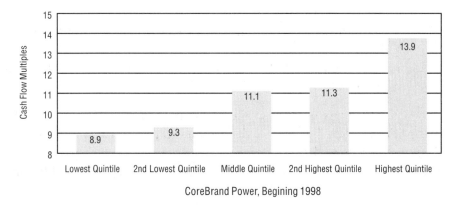

Based on 400 companies with 80 represented in each bar.

Figure 3.7 *Cash Flow Multiple vs. CoreBrand Power*

order to be included in the model, each factor had to be significant by itself and also significant in combination with the other factors. The model was calibrated using three years of data: 1996, 1997, and 1998.

Of most importance, of course, is how stock price change varies with the difference between the actual and this calculated normal level of the cash flow multiple. As Figure 3.8 shows, stock prices increased on average almost 30 percent during the next year for the 80 companies whose cash flow multiple in 1997 was well below the normal level calculated for that year. The 80 companies for which the cash flow multiple was most above the norm on average showed a 6 percent stock price decrease. Thus, results showed that stock prices did tend to be strongly affected by the relationship between actual and normal CFM, at least for that year.

Other factors, psychological as well as financial, influence stock prices as well. One of the most important is stock price momentum. Figure 3.9 shows how stock price change from 1997 to 1998 varied with stock price change from 1996 to 1997. As can be seen, there is a strong relationship in stock price movement during these two years. Because of this, stocks can become overvalued or undervalued, and actual cash flow multiples can be very different in the short term from normal levels.

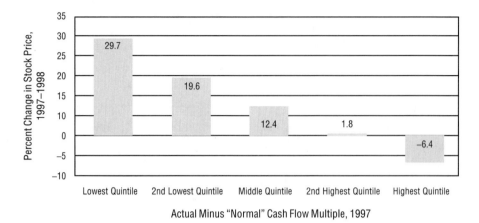

Figure 3.8   *Stock Price Change vs. Actual Minus "Normal" CFM*

Overall Impact on Shareholder Value

Corporate Branding defines change in shareholder value as dividends plus change in stock price multiplied by the number of common shares outstanding. It is assumed in the analyses that dividend policy will be unaffected by the effects that changes in corporate communications have on business results and stock price. Specific quantitative models of the relationships discussed above allow predictions of the results of alternative communications spending plans.

Our researchers have put their quantitative models of these relationships to work helping client companies predict how familiarity, favorability, CoreBrand Power, the cash flow multiple, and stock price are likely to change in the future opposite alternative communications investment plans and expectations of future financial performance.

By looking at how shareholder value—as measured by stock price times shares outstanding—is likely to change with level of advertising investment, an advertising return on investment can be calculated. An optimal advertising level can be calculated by finding the investment level where the next dollar invested in advertising yields less than a dollar improvement in shareholder value for a given time horizon.

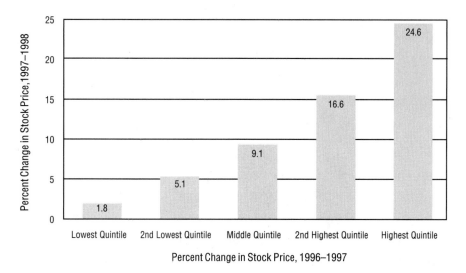

Based on 400 companies with 80 represented in each bar.

Figure 3.9 *Stock Price Change vs. Previous Year Price Change*

Across the Corporate Branding database companies, the analyses indicate that for every ten companies, about three are overspending while seven are underspending at current advertising investment levels. These analyses can prove insightful in helping determine communications spending strategy for publicly traded corporations interested in maximizing shareholder value.

This research gives clear, compelling evidence to conclude that corporate/global image is an important strategic factor that needs to be properly managed if shareholder value is to be maximized in the long run.

Ten Key Points to Review and Remember

1. Corporate communications directly impact corporate image and brand recognition, which in turn helps develop preference and sales.

2. There is a positive association between corporate advertising and "CoreBrand Power," which is a measure of corporate image combining familiarity and favorability.

3. A heavy investment in advertising usually improves familiarity with the company.

4. Advertising investment also usually improves favorability.

5. Research shows that, all other things being equal, companies that improve corporate image grow sales revenue faster than those that do not, resulting in improved earnings and cash flow over the longer term.

6. Share of sales (i.e., market share) tends to move toward CoreBrand share over time, although there are exceptions to this.

7. Research demonstrates that CoreBrand Power has a statistically significant relationship with relative sales growth, and that image is a strong second-level determinant of relative sales growth.

8. Share of voice is a slightly weaker factor than share of CoreBrand Power but is still statistically meaningful in driving sales share change.

9. By looking at how shareholder value—as measured by stock price times shares outstanding—is likely to change with the level of advertising investment, an advertising return on investment can be calculated.

10. Corporate/global image is an important strategic factor that needs to be properly managed if shareholder value is to be maximized in the long run.

4

Cultures, Values, and More

GLOBALIZATION MEANS A good deal more than merely selling or producing overseas. Many factors, including corporate strategy and performance, mergers and acquisitions, accounting and reporting, and the growing scrutiny of corporate, legal, and cultural behaviors around the world, contribute to a highly complex global perspective. To handle such an involved organization successfully, senior management should be both culturally and nationally diverse.

Globalization presents a number of challenges. Keeping the global communications network involved is certainly one of them: trying to span time zones and cultural and language barriers, and involving the communications professionals, whether they are on the agency side or the corporate.

This becomes a series of one-on-one relationships with individuals around the world. Many times a U.S.–headquartered company may say to its international concerns: "We have got a new corporate branding program and here are the rules. Implement them at all your locations." The local people, wherever they are based, will often only look at the global branding rules, nod, and put them on the shelf to gather dust.

The thing to do is to involve individuals, regardless of nationality, and get them to buy in, so that whatever happens is not mere lip service but real implementation. Take it to the next level, rather than simply saying: "We have a program; here's how it works." Go beyond that. Actually work at the local level. In other words, your branding program should be designed to work globally in all local situations.

As a multinational corporation, you operate in many different places. As a global organization, however, everywhere is your home. Difficult barriers can be posed by local culture, language, governmental regulations, and even religion. Therefore, it's vital that you and your company's senior executives find meaning in the cultures and values of others, for they will be your working partners and your markets.

So, to companies that look to globalize, it's important to study and understand each market country and its people carefully. Be sure to consider both differences and similarities. The brand that is successful in one local market will not necessarily be successful as it crosses borders.

Selling Cultural Cachets

L'Oréal is certainly one major company that studies its markets carefully. In a department store in Shanghai, for example, L'Oréal advances its Maybelline brand with an eye-catching show. Few of the women in the admiring crowd realize that the trendy "New York" Maybelline brand belongs to French cosmetics giant L'Oréal.

The French company, valued at $12.4 billion, has a portfolio of international brands that have made it a success in the battle for global beauty markets. Its products range from Redken hair care to Ralph Lauren perfumes to Helena Rubinstein cosmetics.

What's more, L'Oréal has achieved its success through global branding of mature consumer-products companies even when global markets have been shaky. It has done this, according to *Business Week*, by:

> . . . conveying the allure of different cultures through its many products. Whether it's selling Italian elegance, New York street smarts, or French beauty through its brands, L'Oréal is reaching out to a vast range of people across incomes and cultures. That sets L'Oréal apart from marketers such as Coca-Cola Co., which can focus one brand to sell globally . . .

Figure 4.1 *In-Store Display*

Courtesy L'Oreal

> For [CEO] Owen-Jones, the trick will be staying ahead as his rivals seek to play the global branding game. From giant P&G to niche players such as Los Angeles based cosmetic maker Stila, L'Oréal's competitors are hustling to catch up. . . . As Owen-Jones races to expand international sales of his products, he must be careful that his brands don't blur together for consumers.[1]

While many companies seek to homogenize their brands to make them more attractive to a wide variety of cultures, L'Oréal's products have been aimed in a different direction. CEO Owen-Jones wants each of them to exemplify its source country, turning what many marketing experts might consider a restricting factor into a solid marketing virtue. He makes a conscious effort to diversify the cultural origins of his brands, and that approach is more than just a marketing ploy. For L'Oréal, it has also been a successful communications technique in itself, with the company enjoying double-digit growth over the last decade.

L'ORÉAL

Figure 4.2   *Logo*

Courtesy L'Oreal

New Customers for the Golden Arches

Perhaps one of the more interesting challenges of local culture and values has been met by McDonald's Corporation. This familiar brand, already so successful in many parts of the world, has now also won the following of great numbers of consumers to its products, services, and unique ambience in formerly communist Russia.

At this writing, Bloomberg reports that McDonald's plans to open nine new restaurants in Russia, celebrating a decade of serving Big Macs at its first Russian outlet on Moscow's Pushkin Square. This restaurant serves an average of 20,000 customers daily, making it the world's busiest McDonald's.

McDonald's was among the first foreign investors in post-Soviet Russia and was successful from the very first. Thousands of Muscovites and tourists from all over Russia waited for hours in long lines to try American fast food.

By judicious price cutting and local sourcing, McDonald's has kept the crowds coming, despite wars, attempted coups, bank failures, and ruble devaluations. The company, which has so far invested $140 million in Russia, keeps prices low by buying at least 75 percent of its food locally. McDonald's $45 million food processing plant near Moscow supplies meat and pies to its Russian restaurants as well as to 17 other countries. When the ruble plunged initially, McDonald's met the challenge by adding cheaper, locally made, traditional Russian items to its menu, such as soup and cabbage salad.

McDonald's currently employs 5,000 workers in Russia and encourages a growing middle class by promoting managers from behind cash registers. Students are employed part-time and earn a starting salary of about 20 rubles, or 70 cents, per hour.

REFLECTING GLOBAL NEEDS AND TASTES

As successful as they may be domestically, some products need to be adapted to make it in the global market. In 1998, for example, GM bypassed Detroit and sent their new Cadillac Seville to the Frankfurt International Auto Show in Germany. It was the first time General Motors had ever launched a Cadillac abroad.

Peter Levin, director of brand development at Cadillac, explained that the company wanted to send a message that Cadillac was taking the European market more seriously. The new cars were also allocated to help the company's European distributors realize the opportunities created by that launch. The move worked; Seville's European sales increased 60 percent over the prior year.

GM had sold overseas for several years, and Cadillac was earmarked as "global," which meant elevating brand recognition and crafting a global Cadillac image. "We were competing against other global luxury brands, so we knew that going global would also strengthen home market sales," Levin said.[2]

Cadillac has always been a primarily domestic brand targeted toward a very traditional customer with traditional values, customers that tended to be at least 55 years old. But Cadillac's global customer has a younger demographic, possesses strong individualism and confidence, and is forward thinking.

The new Cadillacs are designed and built to reflect global needs and tastes. For example, the new Seville is under five meters long, an important advantage for parking in Europe and Japan. It is available in both right- and left-hand drive models. In France, Italy, and Germany, Sevilles are powered by six-cylinder and diesel engines—in addition to a traditional V-8—and they have more of the understated look that is favored in Europe.

Global marketing materials still feature the well-recognized Cadillac logo, as well as the pillars upon which GM has built its brand: ingenious technology, expressive design, and a personalized ownership experience. Advertising and product sheets are adapted for each country.

George Cohen, McDonald's senior chairman in Russia, claims his biggest task, once given permission to open their first restaurant, was teaching the glum-faced local staff to smile. "It was the height of the Cold War and it was a direct conflict between Karl Marx and Adam Smith," he says. "Since then, the entire thought process has changed and it's much easier to do business."

A Seamless Culture

A common thought process, a common understanding, and acceptance of cultures across borders is necessary to any successful globalization. P. J. Kalff of ABN AMRO Bank has noted: "We need to introduce a set of corporate values and mission across several cultures and product lines—100,000 employees in 72 countries. It is so important to have a common culture. Are we all feeling that we share the targets and ambitions of our future? We have to make sure that we are all working for the same bank. We have got to get people to believe in it. It takes constant attention."

Without a distinctive culture, a company may lose focus and direction, but without a seamless culture it risks losing global effectiveness. Creating that seamless culture can be a problem. Allan Freedman, CEO of Fortis, Inc., has found that "the words echoed in our value statements are probably similar and adhered to more or less within the group. But the cultures are incredibly different. I find that where we get into trouble is always on a cultural point that's never spoken. It's the implicit cultural conclusion or assumption that one or the other side makes that takes you so far down the road before you've even figured it out."[3]

Little Things Mean a Lot: 1

Differences in cultures and national values present all sorts of major challenges to companies seeking to build a global brand. A surprising number of things can derail you. Language, as you might imagine, can be an imposing barrier. So can legal restrictions and political implications. But comparatively little things, too, like time zones and currencies, can prove sizable stumbling blocks that call for special attention.

Even the use of a particular color in corporate design. MasterCard looked to change its logo slightly, putting the familiar yellow and red circles with their white type onto a new control background. But what color should the background be? Choice was limited because Master-Card operates in every country in the world, and thus is specially restricted by what the message of color implies. It couldn't use green, for example, because that had religious connotations in the Middle East. Other colors had their own problems. MasterCard ended up using a shade of blue, considered a culturally neutral color.

A corporate name may also pose problems. For example, there is a tendency in some languages to shorten the brand MasterCard to Master. Sony was first called Tokyo Tsushin Denki before being renamed in 1958. The late Akio Morita, cofounder of the company, wrote in *Made in Japan*: "We wanted a new name that could be recognized anywhere in the world, one that could be pronounced the same in any language." Sony is now, of course, one of the world's most esteemed and accepted brands.

Little Things Mean a Lot: 2

The following story was first published in *Advertising Age* and underscores the point that communication is the key element of branding and the backbone of a global branding strategy:

> The newly promoted global advertising manager for a brand of toothpaste for children was puzzled. The highly successful ad campaign which had boosted sales in the U.S., Canada, Europe, and Australia was not well-received by the folks in the Bangkok office.
>
> "Too American" they kept repeating. . . . So he showed them the French and U.K. versions of the campaign. Still, they were uneasy, and, as politely as their Thai education allowed, they were telling him that the campaign would not work in their country. . . . It had to do with the "pat on the head" mnemonic device which was at the center of all the executions.
>
> That scene, which closed all commercials in the campaign, was designed to express the parent's appreciation for the good brushing the child had done with the toothpaste. But—one does not touch the head of another person in many Asian countries.

Did the young ad manager thus lose his chance for creating a global brand by running afoul of cultural values in Asia? Not at all.

Advertising Age went on to explain: "A global brand is one which is perceived to reflect the same set of values around the world. In the example of the children's toothpaste, the 'pat on the head' is only an execution device to express the parent's appreciation for the child's action, and corresponds to a set of brand values such as: 'Likes children and helps them to be more self-reliant in taking care of their hygiene; is appreciative of the concern parents have for their children's hygiene,' etc."[4]

So if a communication device does not work as well in one market as in others, it can—and should—be replaced with a device that communicates the values that make up the heart of the desired global branding strategy. First, however, the global marketer needs to prepare a thorough and sustainable brand strategy, listing all the particular character traits intended for the brand. Then, to ensure both consistency of message and autonomy of local management, the company's branding team should direct and teach—always sensitively—proper communication of the brand.

A Common Mission

It takes time and a good deal of understanding to build effective relationships with colleagues around the world. They will undoubtedly have different approaches to business. Before a global team can run smoothly, everyone has to learn how well the others in the group grasp the language, appreciate cultural and political requisites, and understand local business customs. Determine these things at the outset or risk offending some people, leaving others behind, and establishing ground rules few can live with.

But just how to meet and grapple with these challenges? Before Hoechst's merger with Rhône-Poulenc, Jürgen Dormann, its chairman, was quoted as saying: "First, we need cultural change. All employees should work in international teams or on international projects. That doesn't simply mean speaking a foreign language; it also means cultural sensitivity and overcoming national paradigms. At Hoechst we promote the international exchange of managers at group level. The bond of common nationality [is] replaced by a common professional mission."[5]

Even if the corporate vision is clearly stated and disseminated throughout your organization, you still must keep focusing on it. You

GAMBLING ON GLOBAL

The move from being merely international to truly global is momentous by any standard. For example, pressured, at least in part, by big international retailers such as Wal-Mart Stores, Inc., Procter & Gamble began rolling out an aggressive global marketing blitz. *This* was a major shift in both company philosophy and organization. P&G was changing from a country-by-country marketing arrangement to one that established seven global business units, organized by product category, such as beauty care, baby care, and so forth. Its corporate goal was to double net sales to $70 billion by the year 2006.

P&G knew that the plan would take as much as two years to implement and depended heavily on increasing market share and sales volume in international markets—many of which were then reeling from economic instability.

To prepare for the plan, top executives, including then CEO, now chairman, John E. Pepper, visited the CEOs of a dozen major companies, seeking advice. Among them, Pepper went to Jack Welch at General Electric to learn how the company streamlined global marketing. He also persuaded Hewlett-Packard Company's then CEO Lewis E. Platt to share enough secrets about new product development to make an instructive video for P&G staffers. This unprecedented road trip led to a shuffling of the P&G hierarchy and a new product-development process designed to speed innovative offerings to the global market.[6]

need to get all your people to buy in to the vision, wherever they're located. You need to hear how they perceive what you say because it will be interpreted in varying ways.

Conference Board research indicates that many global-thinking American and European corporations look especially to broaden the horizons of their own nationals by means of foreign assignments, group planning sessions, audit procedures, informal meetings, and publications. It imparts an awareness of the need for understanding local conditions and for matching them to the corporation's global plans. Without this rapport there can be no true globalization, thus the insight of nonnationals at all levels of the corporate operation becomes essential. Only a few years ago it may have seemed satisfactory to train managers and employees merely to learn and accept the nature of overseas marketplaces; today it's absolutely necessary for all employees to focus on marketplace differences and work with them.

Struggles over Culture

What is the difference between corporate culture and global culture? Whether you're a local, regional, national, or global company, corporate structures may be very similar. More complex are the cultural issues, which can vex a sole-proprietorship or a company with thousands of employees. The only difference is in scale. It's the cultural issues that count and require your full comprehension, whatever your company's size.

Culture implies a great deal more than national or local customs. For one thing, it can also mean differences in executive style. A case in point is the Daimler-Benz and Chrysler merger. When Daimler-Benz A.G. merged with Chrysler Corporation, Thomas T. Stallkamp, president of Chrysler, was rumored, in Detroit at least, to become the president of the new company, DaimlerChrysler A.G., eventually to rise to chairman.

But in ensuing weeks it appeared that Stallkamp was only president of the DaimlerChrysler Corporation, which was in fact the former Chrysler operations, and did not even control the American divisions of DaimlerChrysler A.G.'s Mercedes and commercial truck subsidiaries.

The handwriting was on the wall for those who would read it. After a meeting of the corporation's predominantly German supervisory board, it was announced that the 53-year-old Stallkamp would retire at the end of the year.

A quiet, even gentle man, Stallkamp's hallmark at Chrysler had been his willingness to trust others absolutely, but his easygoing manner apparently did not impress some of his German colleagues. "He wasn't willing to fight for turf," said one supporter. He just wasn't willing to buy into the Daimler culture, and it seems to have cost him dearly.

The *New York Times* reported: "Gerald C. Meyers, a former chairman and chief executive of the American Motors Corporation . . . [and]

among the first to predict cultural clashes when the DaimlerChrysler merger was announced, [commented]: 'We're seeing the beginning of the end of cultural problems. The charade of the merger of equals is starting to fade and the stark reality that one company has bought another has become clear.' "[7]

In an interview with the *Wall Street Journal*, DaimlerChrysler CEO Jürgen Schrempp reflected on the multicultural nature of his company: "I want an American to stay an American. And a German should stay a German. And don't forget—we also have Australians, South Africans, Mexicans, Brazilians. If we get them together, then you get the best answers. There are yellow-skinned, black-skinned, white-skinned—different languages all around—and they argue. If that, ultimately, is the spirit of DaimlerChrysler, then we . . . are really multicultural."[8]

Different Issues in Each Market

Communication in the global marketplace must be interactive. The need to articulate company direction, values, and vision is important, but so too is the need to hear and heed the messages of other cultures. The amount of attention paid to such communication can make or break the global effort.

For example, one of the reasons Levi Strauss relies so heavily on local people is that its managers know there are different cultural, economic, and even legal issues in each market. There is also greater audience sophistication in some regions. In others they might focus on building brand awareness.

Tenneco CEO Dana Mead points out that "the American agenda doesn't always translate. The workers we have in our foreign plants have much different personal and governmental agendas than we do. . . . In some languages the notion of profit is completely foreign. In some languages, if there is a word for profit, it has a connotation that's usually negative."[9]

Perception or Reality?

One question recurs: are some cultural differences more perceived than actual? They certainly are with regard to women in the global work force. Alisa Tang writes in the *New York Times*: "Women account for about half of the United States work force, yet only 14 percent of Americans posted abroad are women. But researchers at two universities say the opinion of some American managers—that women cannot be effective overseas—is not shared by either women working abroad or foreign managers."

She cited a survey of 261 women on foreign corporate assigments and 78 of their supervisors—88 percent of them men—in which 60 percent of the American supervisors agreed or strongly agreed that prejudice in some countries prevented women from being effective on the job. Only 10 percent of the women thought so.

In another survey, among 323 managers in the United States, Germany, and Mexico, the Americans were more likely than those in the other countries to see cultural barriers to women abroad.[10]

A Single Ad Campaign

Culture styles can also bear heavily on how a company communicates its brand and image messages across borders. Differences in culture and tradition raise thorny questions, such as: Where does the responsibility for communication leadership lie—at corporate headquarters, regionally, locally? How should the company address such key issues as strategy, creativity, and politics?

As usual, the experts hold divergent viewpoints. Some sort of centrally coordinated advertising effort is often the preferred solution, but this approach is not without obstacles, nor is it the only solution.

A centrally coordinated communications program allows a corporation to control its brand everywhere. National borders don't stand in the way. And the keystone of a global communications program is advertising. With consistent global application, advertising can make a company appear much the same anyplace in the world—not as numerous separate companies with separate agendas.

How can this be achieved? In brief, determine first which characteristics of your key geographical markets are similar. On that basis, you can develop a unified advertising campaign that addresses all issues. Then implement the campaign nationally, using local languages and media.

Easy? Not really. But definitely doable, considering that differences in cultural traditions, language, and lifestyles generally prove resistant to easy categorization. You know what they say: "But it's not like that in *my* country." Obstacles, as you can imagine, are many and varied. Of special concern are those of strategic, creative, political, or legal natures. These may prove problematic but are not insurmountable, if you bear certain principles in mind.

First, you want to promulgate a clear, consistent vision at all times, one reflected especially in your advertising. Everyone involved—in all locales and on all company levels—should understand and keep sight of *why* you're doing *what* you're doing with the advertising. Pay attention to detail. Global advertising can be complex. It can't function by itself, and requires close and constant supervision.

Also make sure that senior management is convinced the advertising will work because without their full support, the program will not succeed. It takes patience, diplomacy, trust, and an open mind throughout the organization to make the system work smoothly and to accomplish desired ends.

Answering Questions

What are the special demands of global advertising, and how should you meet them? There are a number of problem areas. For instance: How do you develop a message that's equally pertinent in a dozen or more countries? How do you select and define those audiences in the first place? How can you be sure your ads are effective everywhere, despite cultural differences when crossing borders? And how do you get all concerned to agree on a coordinated multinational campaign?

Always start by conducting input sessions, both at headquarters and with subsidiaries in multiple geographical markets. There's no better way to develop an in-depth understanding of the geographic similarities and differences between involved markets and audiences. Such local sessions can add much to the building of a strategic foundation for your advertising.

Sessions should cover such topics as national business objectives; buyer characteristics and typical buying patterns; main competitors and their behavior locally; your own market share, position, and image in key market segments; the opportunities and obstacles in these segments; and the target audiences and how to best reach them.

Creative Pitfalls

In preparing your advertising, what are the creative pitfalls to be avoided? For one thing, don't use translators; use local copywriters to make each ad appear and feel like a national original in every country where it runs. But to be on the safe side, be sure to translate their work back. There is always the chance the ad message may have been distorted, either intentionally to pursue some local agenda or unintentionally by simple cultural misunderstanding.

Don't use humor, word plays, or idiomatic expressions. They don't travel well and usually are rendered meaningless in translation. And whatever else you do, never take conditions for granted. There may be cultural or religious factors and/or current events on the table that you are not aware of. One apt example: advertising and other communications in the Middle East cannot show the faces of women. It's a serious religious issue, though one that might not occur to an American or European art director.

Make sure your local people keep their eyes and ears open—and keep *you* informed. Invite them to endorse the communications strategy and creative execution, and to supervise language adaptations and media selections.

Political Implications

The trickiest and most elusive obstacles facing multinational advertising are the political implications that frequently arise. The power of these should never be underestimated. On various corporate levels, groups and individuals may develop different agendas, hidden as well as overt, for your marketing communications. You'll find that a centralized approach can greatly affect—and even upset—the subtle balance of power between central and local levels.

As Tenneco's Dana Mead notes: "There is no political situation as stable as it appears. . . . Politics is a critical factor in so many foreign projects and deals, in so many business processes. Because we're dealing to a great extent with countries and state-owned enterprises where they have controlled economies, they're going through a difficult transition from state-owned to private economies. . . ."

He adds that political strategy is necessary in these areas.

"First, learn the terrain as best you can. None of us is smart enough to really understand everything about these foreign economies and foreign political situations, unless we've lived in them for a long period of time. But try to do the best you can as fast as you can.

Second and most important: when we go in, we start with an exit strategy, and as we invest, as we make political agreements, as we sign contracts, we think about what the exit strategy from this agreement would be."[11]

Legal Quicksand

I have already discussed language use, its significance to branding across borders, and the role it can play in global-oriented board meetings. This is partly a culture issue, but language has its legal aspects, too. In Canada, for instance, all business communication must be in both French and English. That's required by law. If you're designing an instruction booklet, a mailer, or a flyer, it has to be large enough to accommodate a message in two languages. Or, you can prepare two separate versions—one English, one French—as long as you communicate in both languages.

With the registration of companies abroad, there are many legal issues to concern you. Although your brand may be global, each of the local companies in your network is restricted by the limits of local registration. Ciba Specialty Chemicals, for instance, is registered in at least 30 countries around the world. In the United States, the corporate name is Ciba Specialty Chemicals Inc., but in France it's Ciba Specialty Chemicals SA; and in the United Kingdom it's Ciba Specialty Chemicals Ltd., and so forth.

And as a company goes global, it may encounter a slew of currency transactions, valuations, and fluctuations. Ciba, for example, sends out a quarterly release, usually about five pages long, just to describe the currency fluctuations in the markets where it is registered.

High tech, too, presents a variety of possible legal entanglements. Undoubtedly, tomorrow's successful global corporation is on-line today. There is no doubt that E-commerce is the up-to-the-minute way to penetrate borders—a subject covered more extensively in Chapter 6. But just as the Internet makes it easier to sell globally, it also makes it easier, unfortunately, to violate certain local laws.

For instance, a number of countries—Germany, France, Sweden, and Finland among them—have on their books a confusing assortment of consumer protection laws that make it difficult for global companies to treat the European Union as a common market, especially when selling on-line. One affected company is Lands' End, Inc.

The mail order retailer set up shop in Great Britain in 1991 and in Germany in 1996, and also sells its classic chinos and cardigans in other countries by mail order via the Internet. But as Brandon Mitchener noted in the *Wall Street Journal*:

> [The] company is finding reason to question the logic of a global or even pan-European retail presence since running afoul of a German law banning marketing gimmicks such as an unconditional lifetime guarantee—which happens to be one of Lands' End's guiding principles. . . .
>
> Retailers, lawyers, and lawmakers say the Lands' End case raises legal questions relevant far beyond the borders of Germany, or even the EU, as the Internet exposes companies big and small to laws they never anticipated—and the potential for costly cross-border litigation that many smaller retailers probably can't afford.[12]

A sampling of the various consumer protection laws operating in different European Union member countries includes: bans on rebates and other forms of sales promotion; bans on claims about fuel consumption, effect on environmental quality, or the feature of speed when advertising cars; bans on any television advertising aimed at children under 12; a ban on the advertising of toys; and so forth. These, and other rules like them, may not only prove costly to marketers, but could even become insurmountable obstacles to those small and mid-size businesses that wish to go on-line.

Ordering Global Business Ethics

One other formidable challenge facing global corporations is the formulation of business practice standards around the world, including their implementation and monitoring.

Research finds that the shaping of global business ethics codes now involves 95 percent of CEOs, 92 percent of general counsels, and 78 percent of boards of directors. *Chief Executive Digest* writes that formulation entails conducting an organizational analysis, drafting a code of global business conduct, and creating an awareness of the code through training.

Three trends favor the corporate articulation of global business ethics codes:

- Increased North American and European participation in world markets
- The necessary role of an ethical business climate in improving Asian, African, and Latin American prospects for development
- Increased emphasis on corporate and individual conduct as well as on financial performance

The key organizing principles of such global corporate ethics codes are:

- The requirement of fixed reference points. As laws vary from one jurisdiction to another, from one culture to another, main principles are stated in the common language of ethics.
- The utilization of ethical decision-making procedures to enable managers, wherever located, to act in a manner morally consistent with the principles at the core of their corporate identity and brand.
- An employment environment of trust that is free from reprisals for employee decisions and actions taken in good faith.[13]

Global codes now feature common concerns, particularly with regard to contract (e.g., conflict of interest) and legally mandated (e.g., sexual harassment) ethics standards. Many companies also require supplier, vendor, or joint venture partners to comply with certain provisions of their codes, thus calling for substantial resources to be devoted to worldwide code vigilance and reinforcement.

In addition to the problems presented by the formulation of viable global business practice standards—along with the challenges of cultural, language, and legal barriers—there is one other major obstacle to successful globalization: the scarcity of enough suitable global talent to do the job, which will be covered in the next chapter.

Ten Key Points to Review and Remember

1. Globalization involves more than merely selling or producing abroad. Many kinds of obstacles must be overcome concerning culture, language, and legal issues.

2. Without strong, one-on-one relationships between corporate headquarters and local managers, global branding rules are often ignored on local levels. Individuals, wherever based, must be encouraged to buy in so that the branding program will work in all locales, in all situations.

3. Some products need to be adapted to succeed in a global marketplace.

4. It is important to introduce a common set of values and mission across both border and product lines in order to create a common, seamless culture.

5. At the outset, before the global team can run smoothly, all members have to learn how well the others grasp the language and appreciate cultural requisites; otherwise they risk establishing ground rules few are able to live with.

6. Culture implies a great deal more than national or local customs; it can also mean differences in executive style.

7. Communication in the global marketplace must be interactive. Local people may have different cultural, developmental, economic, and even legal perspectives, and the American agenda doesn't always translate.

8. To meet the special demands of global advertising, one should first develop an in-depth understanding of the similarities and differences between involved markets, conducting special input sessions both at headquarters and with subsidiaries, and covering such topics as national business objectives, buyer characteristics, and competition.

9. A variety of advertising and consumer protection laws may not only prove costly to marketers, but could even present insurmountable obstacles to small and mid-size businesses that wish to go on-line.

10. The formulation of business practice standards around the world is a formidable challenge facing global corporations.

5

Talent: The Real Global Challenge

GLOBALIZATION IS ABOUT linking world economies with new markets. But it also concerns a new kind of competitive environment. You may never have heard of your new competitors, but whatever, whoever, and wherever they may be, they will utilize the global network—as well as a full arsenal of marketing tools available to them—to challenge you. Their labor costs and related problems may be different, and they may work from a different kind of capital base, but suddenly they will confront you and try vigorously to take over your marketplace.

The successful global company realizes that the new technology must be well leveraged. It also knows that competition will rely increasingly both on that technology and on the powerful asset of the knowledge and abilities to be found in its people. Leading companies often may be distinguished by having the best human resources, and many even believe that the only true competitive advantage a company has is its employees. Indeed, employee performance is at the core of business performance, but how many global corporations fully exploit the resource of human capital?

A War for Talent

Professor Nitin Nohria of the Harvard Business School has written that "talent now is global. . . . If the best companies are defined by having the best human capital, especially in a world in which human performance is at the heart of corporate success, then . . . how many companies are taking advantage of this much more distributed human capital? . . . There's a war for talent being fought—globally. And the winners of the next generation will be the people who win this war."[1]

Before going further, it should be emphasized that the "war for talent" is domestic as well as global. Even in the U.S. most companies take a casual and even disconnected approach to building human capital. Recruiting, training, and retaining the highest quality workers is the biggest challenge facing many companies today, and as in anything else, success will belong to those who seize the opportunity with vigor and creativity.

Already I see reform measures being taken by many global-minded companies, not only to find the talent required for success, but to hold on to it. For one thing, executive recruiters are proliferating, with more than 1,000 now in the Silicon Valley alone. And bosses are loosening their traditional iron grip on company rules and regulations in order to keep employees happy.

Plenty of Perks

Relaxed dress codes—which in many firms extend casual Friday throughout the week—title inflation, free lunches, day care, in-house gyms and trainers, and increased health care benefits are some of the perks offered to attract and hold on to superior employees. J.P. Morgan has even set up a separate technology business in Cambridge, Massachusetts, to help in its efforts to recruit top tech graduates.

Banks and other professional firms have always had revolving doors, but these days they seem to be set on exit only. Profit-making New Economy companies such as Microsoft and Oracle, and even established Internet firms such as Excite, find it difficult to halt the departure of their best and brightest to newer Internet startups. Disney, for example, has been heavily raided for its talent.

Global expansion is only one drain on the available work force. There are thousands of new firms on the scene, with more coming each year. They grow quickly and require a continual inflow of quality employees on all levels. Even business schools are struggling in this battle for talent.

Thus, educated, trained people are the real key to a corporation's global success. But finding the right people available and placing them in the right locations with the proper mind-sets is an increasingly difficult and complicated task. It is often the overlooked ingredient for success in the global economy. Finding talent that is knowledgeable, experienced in the technical details of business, sensitive to cultural and other local differences, and competent to carry out the assignment is today's real global challenge.

Unfortunately, not enough American companies focus on this. The challenge for the company that looks to globalize is to establish an infrastructure that allows it to do so and at the same time have the good sense and humility to recognize that although people are different all over, Americans are not necessarily superior.

Distance Education

David Light points out in the *Harvard Business Review* the tremendous need for relevant education in many parts of the world:

> Look at Africa, and you see bountiful natural resources, large labor pools, and untapped markets—a land rich in business potential. But if you want to actually set up operations on the continent, you face a forbidding obstacle: Only 3 percent of 18- to 25-year-olds enroll in college, and few have any business experience.
>
> Now, however, that obstacle appears to be shrinking. Distance education—the use of sophisticated communication technologies to connect geographically dispersed teachers and students—is emerging as an efficient way to bring academic courses and training programs to Africa. One good model, the World Bank's African Virtual University, is already up and running.
>
> The AVU enables students in 16 African countries to take courses and seminars taught by professors from universities around the world. . . . Students are able to talk with the instructors in real time using standard phone lines.[2]

Economic change can't bypass this long-neglected continent forever. For those who can envision the many possibilities of distance education and see its potential contribution to the marketplace, the World Bank's virtual university may serve as a useful means of training a vast labor pool of African workers.

Clear Communication

Many of the major global corporations have well-developed human resource programs, headed by experienced HR experts. Such companies are often highly attuned to and experienced at working with labor unions and international statutory requirements. They are also generally the first to adopt new approaches to organizational effectiveness and high-performance work practices.

Line and HR executives agree that developing tomorrow's leaders while recruiting and retaining a quality work force are major objectives for global success. The three most critical competencies are the ability to facilitate and implement change on a global scale, cross-cultural leadership skills, and a global business understanding.

Meeting these objectives is especially dependent upon clear communication—not merely from the CEO, but from company leaders on all levels. Any successful global human resource strategy must be founded on the ability to communicate basic needs and/or changes in corporate values and vision as well as in company policies and know-how.

A Shrinking Pool of Skilled Talent

Line and human resource executives also agree that two of the most important global business issues are changing employee expectations about work and a shrinking pool of skilled talent.

There are, of course, any number of obstacles that might contribute to a company's lack of success in the global marketplace. A shortage of capital, imperfect technology, a lack of markets, and weak distribution are a few. The obstacle that seems most potentially dangerous is a lack of trained and motivated human resources—resources directed by clear, powerful messaging, and that know, in turn, how to utilize such communication themselves to achieve desired aims.

The alert, forward-looking CEO recognizes the value of human capital. He or she knows that a resource of able, loyal, and creative employees is the true key to corporate success. And the CEO must be a bridge between that resource and the company's customers, investors, and suppliers. In other words, the CEO must use his or her experience as a leader both to inspire the spirit and enthusiasm of the employees and to build and uphold company reputation in the global marketplace.

Jim Kelly, chairman and CEO of UPS, stating that "people are the living embodiment of the corporate brand," goes on to say that "employers neglect this human side of competitive advantage . . . at their own peril."

Kelly offers three "people principles" as the key to creating cultures that enable employees to embody their brands:

- Be the boss
- Walk a mile in the customer's shoes
- Spread your loyalties

By "being the boss," Kelly means empowering employees with equal parts of authority and accountability. He says: "Give employees reasonable freedom to make decisions on their own, and also make them accountable for the consequences of those decisions. In effect, this will make employees more like owners of their own particular area of the company. They will soon see a direct connection between performance and rewards."[3]

Walking a mile in the customer's shoes, the second principle, is the natural outgrowth of an ownership culture. The company must create a mind-set that encourages employees to fit their jobs and work processes to the customer's needs. To do that, it's necessary to establish both formal and informal means of assessing customer satisfaction.

By acting on customer feedback, the company can follow the third principle: spread your loyalties. In other words, companies need to earn loyalty from their employees, and in turn to expect employees to earn the loyalty of their customers. Kelly points to a recent study by Walker Information and the Hudson Institute in which nearly a fourth of American companies were found ineffective at fostering employee loyalty. According to the study, only 24 percent of employees say they are "truly loyal" to their employers and plan to stay with them for at least two years. The study indicated that employers were dropping the ball on such issues as concern, fairness, and trust, rather than on pay and job satisfaction.

The point to be taken is that companies have to do a better job of earning the loyalty of employees. Only then can we reasonably expect employees to extend the same kind of loyalty to customers.

Roadblocks to Success

It seems obvious that developing capable leaders and recruiting and retaining good and loyal workers are major objectives for global success. The greatest roadblocks on the road to globalization include insufficient:

- International experience at headquarters and in the managerial pool
- Talent available in new markets
- Capacity to build and train the local work force and management team
- Understanding of local cultures

Finding technologically trained people has been a problem when companies try to operate with local citizens and to build a local business. A shortage of talent is generally accepted as the number one obstacle to seizing global opportunities.

In *Race for the World*, consultants at McKinsey & Co. write: "CEOs and top managers in every industry identified talent as an important— if not the most important—constraint. Overwhelmingly, managers agreed that they do not have enough leaders to drive their global businesses. They affirmed repeatedly that the difference between failure and success in a given market is almost entirely due to managerial talent. Furthermore, nearly two-thirds of the managers interviewed volunteered that they had real difficulties developing and retaining local talent."[4]

Thus, as we look at global investments, it's not capital, it's not technology, it's not machinery, it's not markets, it's not distribution that determines success; it's people. Or rather, it's often a *lack* of people that prevents a company from capitalizing on opportunities presented overseas. There just may not be enough skilled human resources to cope with all the global challenges.

The Biggest Constraint

What can stop the New Economy from going global? According to Michael J. Mandel, writing in *Business Week*:

> The biggest constraint on the spread of the New Economy globally will not be commodity inflation or product shortages. Rather, the main problem will be finding enough highly skilled and computer-literate workers to staff rapidly growing information industries. . . .
>
> It will be necessary to draw on the enormous supply of college-educated workers in countries such as India and China. . . . Indian universities turn out 122,000 engineers every year, compared with 63,000 in the U.S. And engineers comprise some 40 percent of China's enormous crop of annual graduates.
>
> The growth of the U.S. high-tech industry has been fueled by a steady flow of highly educated immigrants and foreign students. Between 1985 and 1996, foreign students accounted for two-thirds of the growth in science and engineering doctorates at U.S. universities.[5]

An Increase in Expatriates

The dearth of skilled, home-grown managerial talent is causing global-minded companies to place increasing numbers of nationals from outside the headquarters country in top-level positions. In addition, many companies are utilizing strategic staffing plans to ensure that they bring local citizens whenever possible into managerial positions, with international team-building a pivotal issue. There is usually also a corresponding effort made to employ local vendors and contractors.

Having a labor force that is adaptable in the ways of the world in this global age isn't a luxury; it's a competitive necessity. It should come as no surprise that nearly 80 percent of mid-size and large companies currently send professionals abroad—and many of these plan to increase the number they have on assignment overseas.

CEOs initiating globalization efforts report that they have to work especially hard to acquire the talented, experienced executives needed to build the corporate knowledge base. Their companies often rely heavily on expatriates—especially at the start—and the number of employees taking on foreign assignments is growing.

Too often, however, a company may focus on a candidate's technical abilities and gloss over his or her ability to adjust to a new corporate and/or social culture. Some experts believe that an inability to adapt is the single most prevalent cause for overseas assignment failure.

This lack of resilience may be charged to a number of factors. Robert Freedman of Towers Perrin submits: "For some expats, business styles clash; the shortcomings of local backup talent is too frustrating. For others, unhappy children may affect job performance; a working spouse who can't find meaningful local employment may be miserable or won't make the move at all. Some companies relocate employees only at an early stage in their careers, or later, when they're 'empty nesters.' "[6]

Remember, too, that many potential expats aren't necessarily interested in becoming expats. They don't want to move overseas; they weren't hired to be that mobile. The world has changed dramatically since they were hired 20 years ago. How should companies deal with that?

Moving successfully within your own business milieu and culture does not mean that you can operate successfully in another. Studies indicate that companies look for the same basic characteristics in their expats: in particular, an ability to communicate, wide sociability, cultural adaptability, broad-minded positioning, and a cooperative style of exchange and dealing.

A Basic Human Resources Strategy

To meet their goal of recruiting a local work force and management team, some companies find they must improve the educational and technical capacities of the areas in which they operate.

For example, Wayne Allen, retired chairman and CEO of Philllips Petroleum, says Phillips has a human resources strategy that it applies to all its operations: "Hire the best people, train and develop them, praise and recognize their performance, and pay competitively and provide jobs and opportunities that are both challenging and rewarding. . . ."

While some programs are uniform throughout the company, many are tailored to the regions where Phillips operates, in order to accommodate cultural differences that exist from country to country.

When Phillips made plans to develop a new field in the South China Sea, one of its priorities was to train its Chinese employees to take over the management of the operation. The company had three specific strategies:

- Overcome cultural differences
- Train employees in the latest technologies
- Train employees in business processes

Former CEO Wayne Allen offers the details:

By following these we knew we could position our Chinese employees to advance in their jobs and assume greater responsibility over day-to-day operations. In 1998 we placed a Chinese national in charge of our $600 million Xijiang operation. . . .

We knew little about Chinese culture. To better understand it, we asked our Chinese employees to conduct orientation classes for our expatriate work force. They taught their U.S. counterparts local customs and traditions, the etiquette of the region, and nuances of behavior and language.

At the same time, we insisted that our expatriates study the language, not only to show respect for their Chinese colleagues, but also to develop a relationship that could not be achieved through an interpreter.[7]

One of the Itochu Corporation's corporate identity program's goals was to transform a highly matured corporate culture into one that was much more challenging internally. The company recognized that its initial corporate culture of risk taking, positive thinking, and self-motivation had been diluted and needed to be revitalized.

As to which ingredient of that corporate identity program is most important, Minoru Murofushi, president and CEO, declares: "Without question, the most critical part of the program is the effective development of our human resources. This is the key to realizing our vision. The difficulty, of course, is that nowhere is there an established 'best practices' model to guide our management processes, our practices, and systems safely toward this new world. . . . So we gather the best practices of global management and leadership models from both the West and East."[8]

Ten Key Points to Review and Remember

1. What are you doing to exploit fully the resource of quality human capital?

2. Today there is a global war for talent, and the winners of this war will be tomorrow's most successful corporations.

3. To recruit and retain quality employees, many global-minded corporations are offering a wide variety of perks.

4. Sophisticated communications technologies are connecting geographically dispersed teachers and students in order to bring courses and training programs to large, untapped labor pools of African students.

5. The CEO must be the bridge between the resource of able, creative employees and the company's customers, investors, and suppliers.

6. Three "people principles" are the key to creating cultures that enable employees to embody their brands:
- Be the boss
- Walk a mile in the customer's shoe
- Spread your loyalties

7. The greatest roadblocks on the road to globalization are people and culture issues, including insufficient:
- International experience at headquarters
- Available talent in new markets
- Local capacity to build and train work force and management team
- Understanding of cultures

8. Global-minded companies often rely heavily on expatriates, and their number is increasing steadily.

9. Among expats, an inability to adapt is the single most prevalent cause for overseas assignment failure.

10. To recruit a local work force and management team, some companies must improve the educational and technical capacities of the areas in which they operate.

6

The Emerging Global Customer

TODAY'S CUSTOMERS—AND tomorrow's—are a great deal different from the consumers and business-to-business purchasers the world has been used to. Globalization is changing things. So, too, is the advance of technology, the Internet in particular.

The Internet is changing how companies compete, how they approach the global marketplace. The successful companies of the future are on the Internet today and taking full advantage of its potential to initiate new business practices.

And their customers are on the Internet. Without leaving their homes or offices, they travel the world, millions of them every day. Their wants and needs, opinions and beliefs, cross borders and challenge cultures with speed and power. They are on the Web, and so they're global; accessible to all the websites and all the branding messages being delivered via the Internet.

The goal is to keep them coming back. Customer loyalty, domestic or global, doesn't develop overnight. Nor is it won through "attitude" or extravagant promises, flashy images or gimmicky design. Loyalty is developed through a succession of positive experiences customers have with the brand. To your customers, each experience should be satisfying and reassuring.

Even more important, each experience should build momentum in customers' minds, reinforcing your brand as their preferred choice. As experiences accumulate and expectations develop, your brand makes the implicit promise to perform successfully against those expectations.

The experience at Corporate Branding with E-commerce and the Internet supports this. The Corporate Branding website is a primary communications tool and creates many global opportunities. Despite having to deal with various unqualified leads and student inquiries, the Internet delivers a wide scope of useful responses.

Similarly, your website can play a logical role as a central communications resource for your company, conveying not only your brand voice, but its identity and reason for being. It also gives Internet customers greater access to information about your company, its products, and key business issues. It's plain that with high-tech just about everywhere, customers are making good use of it.

Technology Is Omnipresent

Everyone is getting wired. Laptop computers and handheld or desktop devices not only fill the workplace but the home as well. Selling becomes increasingly about relationships—service and advice, more than just booking orders—across borders and around the world. The challenge is to extend people's views beyond their own cultures, their own boundaries—to point out the many ways in which the world is more similar than different.

People who buy electronically are more sophisticated and demanding. They value fast response and want to talk with you only when they need to. The Internet may still be in its relative infancy, but it makes it easy for a customer to move on quickly to the next supplier, should the first one not have the right product, price, or delivery capability.

The message is clear: if you can communicate, you can leapfrog time and space. What we call globalization is driven above all by technology and is changing the world with extraordinary speed. The Internet has changed everything. It's compelled us to think and move faster, and to be more aggressive. But although the medium may be different, the fundamentals still apply. Strong brands are not bought overnight. They are built one experience at a time.

As with any other core business function, on-line brand-building activities must proceed from an explicit, well-defined strategic perspective. They must serve clear objectives. They must promise and deliver value. Above all, they must support and reinforce the brand images and messages delivered to customers in print, broadcast, and other media.

An Absolute Reflection of Your Brand

Your website isn't just a marketing tool or a distribution channel. It's an absolute reflection of everything the brand and company represent. It's where everything—including products and services, customer support, overall attitude and voice—comes together. Design, text, navigation, and functionality should support and reinforce a distinctive brand experience.

Every aspect of a company's website should flow logically from a sound brand strategy. If the website is already up and functioning, that strategy can serve as a filter or standard against which to measure existing work—one that can also guide the development of the site.

There are two basic steps to building distinctiveness on a website:

Step 1: Define the underpinnings of the brand. These underpinnings constitute the strategic backbone of the brand—what we call CoreBrand™ strategy. Such a plan articulates, among other things, the brand's reason for being, what it delivers, what its core focus is, and the voice it uses to communicate.

Step 2: Execute the strategy. Once the strategy is articulated and understood, it's possible to execute it in communicative, navigational, and functional terms: how the site looks and feels to the user, the messages it conveys, the ease of movement from one part of the site to another, the types of E-commerce solutions the site offers, and the built-in banners and links it contains.

Remember: brand strategy is business strategy. The two feed off one another. In the end, brands succeed not because of what companies say about themselves, but because of what they do, how they function, and how successfully they meet customers' needs and expectations. So make your brand different; make it relevant; make it credible.

Building an On-line Network

Not only is the Internet being used to build new brands, but, increasingly, to embellish established brands. It is also the obvious means of introducing companies to E-business. By joining the E-economy, they find they can lower prices, add customers, and boost productivity.

With business-to-business transactions rushing to go on-line, the global marketplace becomes more efficient—and inviting. Consider the expansion plans of a number of major globally oriented corporations.

For example, Ford Motor Co., General Motors Corp., and DaimlerChrysler A.G. recently announced that they are abandoning their independent efforts and joining forces to build a business-to-business, $250 billion parts exchange on the Internet. This alliance will greatly speed deliveries and communications to suppliers, business partners, and customers from all over the world.

Detroit's Big Three regard the combined parts exchange as only an initial step toward putting all their business on the Web. Alex Taylor, writing in *Fortune*, said the companies see this exchange "as the foundation of an Internet-based industry that designs and engineers cars faster and better, and eventually builds them to order, delivering them directly to customers within a few days. . . . A fully Web-enabled auto industry—one that not only customizes cars but also eliminates dealers from the equation—could cut the cost of a vehicle. . . .

"The parts exchange represents an unheard-of level of cooperation among the Big Three, and the companies are pushing it with uncharacteristic speed."[1]

It may not be all smooth sailing for the auto-industry exchange, however. *Business Week* commented: "Some sites simply have too many cooks in the kitchen. Covisint, the auto-industry exchange backed by Ford Motor, General Motors, and DaimlerChrysler, has four co-CEOs. The car-makers are such fierce rivals that choosing a name took nearly three months. Similar battles took place over what technologies they should use."[2]

The Web's liberal standards and its global reach make it an ideal arena for conducting business in new ways. And these automotive giants are not the only ones to demonstrate how large corporations can use the Internet to put themselves decisively in the midst of new E-business ecosystems. Sears, France's Carrefour, and Oracle have announced a retail consortium, called GlobalNetXchange, that will bring together as much as $80 billion of annual purchases. Another such retail B2B Web exchange, WorldWide Retail Exchange, includes Kmart, Target, Tesco, Safeway, CVS, and other companies with combined sales of $300 billion.

Other notable examples of corporations that are establishing Internet supply networks for their industries include International Paper, Georgia-Pacific, and Weyerhaeuser (paper); Weirton and Bethlehem Steel (steel); and Johnson & Johnson, Medtronic, and Abbott Laboratories (medical products). There are already literally hundreds of B2B websites that make markets in a particular field. They link buyers with sellers, integrating sourcing, purchasing, and billing for all involved parties. (See Chapter 8 for additional details.)

Like the town square marketplace of long ago, these electronic exchanges bring together buyers and sellers, though in this case they can be thousands of miles apart. Today, a company searching for other companies on the Web can find just the right match for its geographical needs, time constraints, product requirements, and so forth.

Some businesses are slow to move to business-to-business E-commerce. They claim that many of their customers have come to rely on human sales reps. Personal relationships are important, of course, but these companies don't understand that a strong brand, utilized as a powerful beacon, will help align the new selling process with new technologies, and motivate customers, investors, partners, and others.

A Road to Monopoly?

Despite all the possibilities of B2B on the Internet, there is a growing feeling among regulators and some companies in the industries being transformed that such exchanges might become dangerous, monopolistic tools. As of this writing, both the Federal Trade Commission (FTC) and the Department of Justice (DOJ) began investigations of the possible antitrust implications of three of the more prominent exchanges, and the Senate commerce committee had plans to hold hearings.

The FTC review has already helped delay the start of Covisint, the site devoted to the major auto manufacturers. Antitrust worriers fear that companies could use them to rig prices to sellers. They are also concerned that big buyers could gang up on suppliers, either through collective purchasing or through the amplified buying power created by an efficient market.

Even the exchanges could turn into monopolies, with the biggest attracting buyers and sellers alike. Those companies with a winning exchange in one market could conceivably use that power to expand into additional markets.

Up to now, FTC and DOJ inquiries have been fact-finding excursions rather than full-fledged investigations. Nevertheless, the potential still remains for overzealous intervention. Whether the new B2B exchanges will get under way successfully may depend at least in part on the indulgence of the trustbusters.

A Single, 24-Hour Global Market

The creation of multifirm supply networks is only one way the Internet connects buyers with sellers. The trading of stock on-line, for example, is gaining wider acceptance with investors everywhere. In only a few years, the business of trading stock shares will look radically different, with many of the old stock exchanges gone, replaced by new share-trading systems or perhaps merged with others.

According to *The Economist*, The Nasdaq, currently the second-biggest stock market in the world, has formed affiliations with stock exchanges in Japan, Hong Kong, and Canada, among others. The New York Stock Exchange was recently looking into the feasibility of a global equity market that would link exchanges in several countries, including France and Japan, with an aim toward a single 24-hour market where shares of the world's largest blue-chip firms could be traded.

Although the U.S. has recently experienced a bull market, with investors and traders flourishing, it has been predicted by some that the Big Board may be on the way out. Its crowded, noisy trading floor and restrictive rules and practices are turning off some of America's most exciting and attractive New Economy companies, and they are listing on Nasdaq instead.

The NYSE has been slow to make alliances or enter joint ventures with overseas markets. It has not adapted as markets have evolved, although some financial institutions are investing in rivals, such as on-line trading systems. Generally known as electronic communication networks (ECNs), these systems are changing the traditional image of the hectic trading floor, crowded with noisy traders. This is not considered a proper message for today's cyberworld.

But the biggest stock exchange news these days is not about jam-packed floors versus computer screens, but rather about the spread of international partnerships and mergers. Until its recent announcement of a possible linkage with several foreign exchanges, however, the NYSE seemed to have been left out of this current wave of international consolidation. *The Economist* also reported:

> The mergers have been guided by the idea that technology overrides geography. If there is no longer a stock exchange floor, nobody really cares where the matching and execution of orders takes place. A buyer could be in Frankfurt and a seller in Memphis. . . . What is . . . likely is that the big blue chips will hope to benefit from a network of stock exchanges, old or new, that can deliver global trading.
>
> By seeking now to link up with the French, Japanese, and others, the NYSE is implicitly recognizing this. But its cultural resistance both to change and to alliances may still prove a big obstacle. . . . It may be that it gets left behind by the rush to create an integrated world marketplace.[3]

The Internet Century

The Internet, of course, is all over the place—not just in the investment business. AOL's Steve Case has already dubbed this the "Internet Century." He explained: "There is probably going to be more confusion in the business world in the next decade than there has been in any decade, maybe in history. I can't think of any that brought the kind of topsy-turvy change that's starting to happen now, and the pace is only going to accelerate."

Fortune said of Case: "For a year or so, the soft-spoken CEO of America Online has been saying that he wants to build the most valuable, most respected, most important company in the world. He describes AOL's mission this way: 'to build a global medium as central to people's lives as the telephone or television . . . and even more valuable.'"[4]

Case has painted a picture of a giant, customer-oriented corporation, a megaforce in media, communications, retailing, financial services, health care, education, and travel. It will compete with just about every-

AWARENESS ISN'T TRUST

Despite the heavy promotional investment in dot-coms, recent research indicates that, on the whole, consumers still trust the traditional bricks-and-mortar brands more than they do the newer Internet startups. The study, conducted in London by advertising agency Leo Burnett, shows that consumer trust in a brand can fall short even though the awareness of the brand may rank high. Sarah Ellison wrote in the *Wall Street Journal*:

> While brand-building is crucial to the success of any company, just because people recognize a brand doesn't mean they will still use it. In the case of British concerns . . . more consumers said they were likely to purchase from the websites once they knew the name of the well-known parent company. A lot of this is about leveraging trust from one medium to another, moving trust from the off-line to the on-line world. . . .
>
> The study showed people are more likely to trust traditional brands that have been around for years. But putting an off-line brand on-line is sometimes not a good idea, because the company's traditional image may not be appropriate for its Internet identity. So promoting on-line brands is a balancing act between creating a hip new identity that targets the desired audience, and using the power of a traditional brand to support perceptions of reliability and trust.[5]

continued

thing from newspapers, television stations, and phone companies to banks, brokerage firms, auto dealerships, and travel agencies. As a result, interactivity will become increasingly a part of the everyday life of more and more people.

Brand Relationships on the Web

We know that a strong brand involvement builds brand relationships, which in turn demand greater customer loyalty. We also know that loyal customers make a dramatic difference on the business's bottom line. For example, if a company keeps only 5 percent more of its loyal users, the impact on its bottom line can be as much as 50 percent because such customers are so profitable.

There are three basic approaches to the creation and promotion of on-line brands:

- Create an entirely new brand unencumbered by past history

- Leverage the name of the off-line parent company as the name for the new on-line brand

- Create a new brand for the on-line company but make its connection to the more familiar parent company known by means of advertising, public relations, and other corporate communications

Research shows that traditional companies rate high in both brand awareness and brand trust. When asked to rank new Internet brands, awareness ranking is close to that of the traditional companies, but brand trust lags well behind. For those Internet companies backed by traditional brands, the levels of trust and the likelihood that a consumer will make a purchase rise when consumers are told the name of the parent company.

Visa International, an association of 21,000 banks with 880 million payment cards in the market, sees the Internet as a means of building a strong brand involvement with customers, employees, and other stakeholders. To help build customer brand involvement on the Internet, Visa believes there are a number of steps an organization can take:

- Seek ways to provide services or information that reinforce the brand's proposition
- Build in feedback loops so consumers can comment on the website
- Personalize the site rather that just customize it
- Always deliver on promises, in order to build trust

Caroline McNally, Visa's senior vice president, global brand management, has said:

In a similar way, an organization's internal Internet [its intranet] can be used to encourage employee brand involvement by providing updates on the state of the brand, educating them about the benefits of building a brand identity, and informing them about competitive brand activities.

But Visa recognizes that the Internet is open to all and that it will be difficult to sustain brand loyalty when competitors, possibly with more tempting offers, are only a mouse click away.

Being different, though, is not enough. McNally points out: "Successful brands will provide the extra trust needed to reassure us that what we're buying on-line will meet our expectations."[6]

Two Types of Brands

Philip Evans and Thomas S. Wurster write of two types of brands. For those involved in E-business, the differentiation is worth noting:

> Manufacturers use branding all the time to communicate rich, product-specific information to their consumers. But there are two different types of brands, and we believe that one is far better suited to E-commerce than the other.
>
> Some companies attempt to convey facts or beliefs about product attributes through branding. Sony, for example, persuades consumers to believe that it will deliver superior technology, high manufacturing quality, and miniaturization at a modest but warranted price premium. Each of these things is a belief about Sony products—perhaps true, perhaps not.
>
> Other marketers use branding to communicate an experience: feelings, associations, and memories. "Coca-Cola" cannot be paraphrased as a set of propositions about the drink. The brand is the taste, the curvy bottle, the logo, and the set of emotional and visual connotations that the drink carries by merit of a century of advertising.
>
> Rich information channels have very different effects on brand-as-belief and on brand-as-experience. To the extent that a brand is a matter of belief, the brand message is fundamentally a "navigator" message.[7]

According to Evans and Wurster, a navigator message is one from a product supplier or retailer, designed to help the customer "navigate" among many possible choices to find just the right product. Navigators create "navigational" tools, that is, everything from branding and advertising to relationship building and merchandising. These tools help customers avert the complexities of a comprehensive search to find products they're willing to buy.

JANE MACKIE ON DEALING WITH A LOT OF DIFFERENT PEOPLE

Taken from the author's recent interview with Jane Mackie, vice president marketing, Sheraton Hotels & Resorts Inc.

Our most global brand is Sheraton Hotels and Resorts. We expanded Sheraton outside the United States in 1967, our company being started in 1937. Quite early in our corporate history we were already expanding overseas. We now have large divisional offices in Brussels for the European division, Cairo for the African, India for the Middle East division, Singapore for the Asian-Pacific division, and Buenos Aires for the Latin American division. Sheraton, in the eyes of the consumer and our employees, is considered as much an Egyptian or French or Argentinean brand as it is an American one.

Culturally, we've been very fortunate. It's a name that doesn't have a definition, if you will, in any specific language, and it's had a very universal and global life. (Incidentally, it would be my advice that any brand that has the intention of being global someday should start the process as soon as possible to make that brand multinational.)

We drive global brand strategy, to a large extent, centrally, with implementation done in each division and with some customization at each divisional level. Business decisions are made on all levels, regional and local as well. Our customers are obviously not necessarily located in the same place geographically. Therefore when we are marketing Israel as a travel destination, for example, we promote that heavily in the United States and Europe.

Advertising is generally developed by our divisional offices, with centralized media purchasing by our global advertising agency, DDB. We do have some regional or local hotel market advertising and promotions.

To determine the effectiveness of our branding communications, we conduct benchmark studies among our key audience segments.

continued

That would be the individual business traveler, the individual leisure traveler, and the meetings customer. We also conduct studies to measure their satisfaction, and position it year by year between ourselves and our competitors.

In addition, we have a guest satisfaction study. It is a key indicator—how satisfied the guests were when they checked out—and is an indication of loyalty and their intent to return.

In our industry, customers are global. They expect a certain similarity, but they also want to know that they've been in a particular place. They don't want to stay in a Sheraton in Brussels and feel as if they've been at the Sheraton New York. They want a bit of local flavor. It's the same with the employees. They need to embrace the workplace. It should have the appropriate local flavor.

In Europe, 25 percent of our business comes from the United States and about 60 percent are Europeans traveling within Europe. And their needs do differ slightly. It's not just European versus American. A German would have different expectations than, say, someone from Italy. So we must always pay attention to the requirements of the individual customer. These will always differ by culture.

You have to embrace a lot of different cultures. At the same time, it's fine to have a global branding strategy, with certain core benefits and core values of your brand that are global. And then implement local customizations as needed to address individual customer needs, employee satisfaction, and international travelers' expectations.

The idea is that if you buy a Sony, you'll get better technology that weighs less and has higher manufacturing quality. Because the brand in this case is a matter of belief, the brand message is basically a navigator message.

Brand-as-experience is a different story. Barbie, for example, is not a brand defined by Mattel's statements about it or by its product specifications. Rather, Barbie represents a fantasy world for young girls, while at the same time it is a collectible for adults. Mattel invests huge resources in order to create and preserve the consistency with which this fantasy world is presented to the public.

To thrive in a global environment of complex and critical relationships with customers and partners calls for real-time decision-making and quick access to information from many sources. Success depends always on superior communications. The customer's voice drives decisions, and only prudent planning ensures that his or her needs are met or exceeded. Nowhere is this more evident than in the international travel business. Consider Sheraton Hotels.

Take Your World with You

Today's globally oriented CEOs must understand the power of a customer-centric supply chain, know how to optimize it, and appreciate the technologies needed to leverage it throughout their companies. Moreover, they must learn how to cross boundaries to access the crucial information possessed by various trading partners. Not only the Internet, but an ever-growing list of technological advances make such intelligence gathering possible.

The move from wired telecommunications to wireless is particularly significant, considering today's need to cross borders easily and effectively. The growth in the number of mobile phone subscribers has been extraordinary. In 1990 there were just over 11 million worldwide, while today there are almost 400 million. Compare this to only 180 million people using personal computers. By the year 2004 it is estimated that the number of mobile phones throughout the world may well reach one billion, exceeding the number of wired phones. And we haven't even scratched the surface of their potential functionality.

Business Week envisions the following scenario:

> A 15-year-old girl strolls through London's Berkeley Square. Suddenly she hears a beep from her cell phone and looks at the screen. A message sponsored by Starbucks informs her that two friends from her "buddy list" are walking nearby. Would she like to send them an instant message to meet for coffee at the nearest Starbucks around the corner? She merely has to click "yes" on her "smart phone" to send the message. And she gets an electronic coupon worth $1 off a Frappuccino.

From Tokyo to Stockholm to Silicon Valley, telephone companies, software designers, and phone equipment suppliers are all revving up their
strategies for the next technological revolution: wireless access to the
Internet. Already in Europe—and to [some] extent in the U.S.—customers can dial in to receive e-mail, weather reports, and other specialty
packages via their cell phones. . . . A portable and constant link to the
information world could change lifestyles—and offer business opportunities—just as much as the Web has up to now.[8]

Adrian Wooldridge commented in *The Economist*: "Mobile phones
are rapidly becoming ubiquitous; now they are about to become multi-
purpose, too, offering everything from Internet access to an organized
life. . . . If the wired revolution changed the way we think about distance, the wire*less* revolution is changing the way we think about place.
. . . It is helping people bring [location] under control, allowing them to
overcome its limitations as well as making it easier to enjoy its benefits.
. . . Motorola says that mobile phones allow you to 'take your world
with you.' "[9]

In actuality, the wireless revolution effectively disposes of the restrictive despotism of locality. One of the biggest disadvantages of being
born into the world of the poor has been the isolation from modern
communications. This means one is locked into the local economy. But
mobile phones can be great equalizers. They take the latest tools of communication to areas where traditional phone companies cannot reach.

There's no question that technology has become increasingly influential in our lives—both in the workplace and in our consumer concerns. As we have noted, cell phones are now practically obligatory,
while laptops and desktop units proliferate prodigiously. The significance is self-evident: Every year growing numbers of business customers
and consumers are buying electronically. More and more of these E-
sales are global, taking brands across borders with facility and speed.
And as interaction costs go down, small businesses and retailers will be
more likely to participate in the electronic marketplace.

According to *Across the Board*, U.S. on-line advertising hit $2.6 bil-
lion in 1999, a 73 percent jump over the previous year. *E-Marketer*, a
trade publication, predicts Internet ad sales will hit $8.9 billion by the
year 2002.[10]

Gene Koprowski, writing in *Critical Mass*, quotes Forrester
Research as reporting that "2004 revenues are projected to be as much

as $33 billion. . . . The World Wide Web has achieved critical mass as an advertising medium in an incredibly short span of time—faster than radio, and much faster than TV. . . . Who knew that the Internet would be so big?" [11]

Setting Up a B2B Initiative

The growth in technology has persuaded at least one major financial institution to roll out a global initiative by building and hosting transactional E-commerce sites for its business customers. As Philip Clark pointed out in *Ad Age International*, Citibank, "operating in more than 100 countries, has been approaching companies throughout Asia and Europe, and next year will begin pitching companies in the U.S. and Latin America.

"Citibank began rolling out Citibank Commerce several months ago in Singapore, and has recently begun marketing to companies in Australia, Hong Kong, the Philippines, Thailand, and parts of Europe."

Citibank is the first bank to get into the business-to-business site development and hosting marketplace. Until now this has been almost the exclusive territory of technology-oriented companies. But by leveraging its existing financial relationships with business customers, Citibank looks to break into the B2B E-commerce area traditionally enjoyed by high-tech corporations.

This would enable Citibank to offer its 2,300 worldwide business customers assistance in establishing transactional, Citibank server-hosted websites. Its portal sites could include industry breakouts such as chemicals, supply Web homes to Citibank's business clients, and eventually allow the customers of these clients to order products and make payments on-line.[12]

A Common Look and Feel

ITT Industries strives to provide a common look and feel to all of their websites. When I interviewed First Vice President and Director of Corporate Relations Thomas Martin, he noted:

> One of the things we designed, with the help of Landor Associates, was an on-line identity manual that basically takes the fundamentals of the

"It's kind of hard to have a **fishing industry without fish**. That's exactly what happened in Sicily due to industrial pollution. Then we came in and helped mix things up—literally. We designed and provided the big, dependable, submersible pumps and mixers that drive their new water purification process. And once it started operating, the water started coming back to life—fish and all. Hallelujah!"

Zbigniew Czarnota, Research Engineer, Stockholm

OUR FLYGT 4800-SERIES SUBMERSIBLE MIXERS ARE ENGINEERED WITH OPTIMIZED HYDRAULICS FOR EFFICIENCY AND CLOG-FREE OPERATION. THESE MIXERS CREATE THE FLOW SO THAT IT FOLLOWS TANK SHAPE WITH MINIMUM HYDRAULIC LOSSES. NO AREA OF A TANK IS LEFT UNMIXED AND ENERGY CONSUMPTION IS MINIMIZED.

ITT Industries
Engineered for life

Figure 6.1a   *Advertising Preview 1998*

"Hallelujah" Television :30

First a great bullfrog and then a growing number of fish begin to sing Handel's Hallelujah Chorus. The voice of Hal Linden explains why: *"Communities around the world are cleaning up their water with the help of durable pumps engineered by ITT Industries. Hallelujah!"*
A chorus of fish, porpoises, whales, turtles and seals joins in a final chorus until, again, the voice of Hal Linden closes with: *"ITT INDUSTRIES. Engineered for life!"*

Figure 6.1b   *Advertising Preview 1998*

Courtesy ITT Industries Inc.

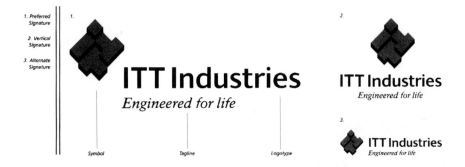

Figure 6.2a   *Basic Guidelines Manual*

Courtesy ITT Industries Inc.

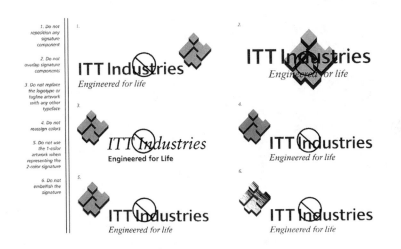

Figure 6.2b   *Basic Guidelines Manual*

Courtesy ITT Industries Inc.

 ITT Industries
Engineered for life

 In Our Hands
Summer 2000
A quarterly newsletter for all employees of ITT Industries

"This is the most significant investment of time, resources and talent in any corporate-wide initiative in the history of our company."

— Vince Fayad, Director, Value-Based Six Sigma

Value-Based Six Sigma
Full Speed Ahead

Up Front

ITT Industries has never committed so many company resources to one initiative, but that's because there's never been an initiative that could promise so much in return. Here's a look at the continuous improvement effort that will leverage our knowledge base and reshape the way we work.

Bob Poresky thought he had seen and heard it all. A 20-year veteran of Goulds Pumps, this senior staff engineer has watched "countless" continuous improvement programs come and go at the Seneca Falls, New York, plant. So he was as amazed as everyone else when a two-hour meeting in mid-March washed away two decades worth of skepticism.

"It was a plant meeting to introduce this new initiative called Value-Based Six Sigma," says Poresky. "Sitting there, I went from apprehension to curious excitement; by the end of the meeting, I was pleased to be a part of it."

Value-Based Six Sigma is a new company-wide continuous improvement effort that — according to ITT Industries Chief Operating Officer Lou Giuliano — is going to

continued on page 2...

Figure 6.3a *Employee Newsletter*

Figure 6.3b *Employee Newsletter*

Courtesy ITT Industries, Inc.

branding work and translates them into website guidelines. We have those guidelines available on-line, so they define Internet colors, typography, and that sort of thing.

Yes, we have a master website, which is ITTIND.com, which can also be accessed by just ITT.com. That gives a reference to all the other websites in the different management companies so that people can access those either way.

[The importance of the E-consumer to us] depends on a variety of factors. We have so many different kinds of products and different kinds of markets that the focus we've had on E-commerce has been very much on a business-to-business basis. And it varies by market.

For example, we're not going to sell jamming equipment for FA-18 fighter aircraft over the Internet. So, for a lot of our defense product services—which accounts for about a fourth of the total company—I think an Internet relationship is going to be pretty remote. Those are highly controlled and in some cases highly classified systems. And they are sold to such a very select group of people that you could practically get them all into one fairly small room. That's your customer base.

ATTAINING SUPERBRAND STATUS

As influential as electronic media is coming to be, today's consumer is not, of course, restricted to it. Some of the old standbys are still very influential. Take *Reader's Digest*, for example. Currently, it has more than 100 million readers worldwide, spanning 48 editions in 20 languages.

PRNewswire reports that since 1999, *Reader's Digest* has taken annual surveys to determine which brands appeal most to Asian customers. For the Asia SuperBrand 2000 survey, a total of 82,000 questionnaires were randomly inserted into the November 1999 issue. To obtain a representative cross section of respondents, questionnaires were distributed in English, Chinese, and Thai editions in six countries including Hong Kong, Malaysia, the Philippines, Singapore, Taiwan, and Thailand.

Participants were asked to name their most preferred brand for 41 categories of products and services covering lifestyle products and daily necessities. The response rate was 7.4 percent, excellent by mail survey standards. Top performing brands received a 2000 *Reader's Digest* Award of Excellence for Outstanding Brand Performance.

The Acer Group, based in Taiwan, attained the Gold SuperBrand status for Asia in the computer category for the second consecutive year. Jerry W.T. Wang, vice president of Acer corporate brand management, remarked: "As this award demonstrates the consistent view of the Acer brand shared by consumers in Asia, we'd like to spread the same strong visibility on a global basis."

Peter Jeffery, regional advertising director of *Reader's Digest Asia*, said: "To reach SuperBrand status, a product must consistently demonstrate success in a wide range of qualities. This survey truly reflects outstanding brand performance for all products listed."

According to *Reader's Digest*, a true SuperBrand needs to display a high level of consumer awareness, trust, and respect, among other qualities. Research takes into account both quantitative and qualitative criteria. The five qualitative categories were quality, value, trustworthiness, strong image, and understanding of consumer needs.

Acer is the world's third largest PC manufacturer, offering a broad range of PC products from industry-leading high-end PC servers and multimedia desktop computers, to notebooks, computer peripherals, and components. Acer is also the leading Internet enabler offering Internet component technologies, devices, and Internet services. These include end-to-end solutions, mobile phones, plasma displays, projectors, wireless communications, and E-corp solutions.

The Acer Group employs more than 33,000 people in 120 enterprises spanning 37 countries worldwide, supporting dealers and distributors in more than 100 countries.

On the other hand, in our pump and valve area we sell to very broad groups of people—people who are buying systems for flood control or water treatment. And we also sell the valves, heating, ventilation, and air-conditioning to contractors who have need for information on our products. They need part numbers, information on system designs, on components. We have done things in our fluid-handling area that we like to call a fluid-handling university. There, people can go into the website and actually identify a system or part of a system or whatever.

In our electrical connector area, which is a company called Cannon, we designed a website where people can go and locate as many as 50,000 part numbers.

A Bridge to E-Business

E-commerce isn't limited to U.S. and European companies. Today a rapidly developing enthusiasm for the Internet is engulfing Asia, a sound portent of a substantial growth in E-business to come, with business-to-business already its fastest growing area.

This enthusiasm for the Internet was certainly reflected by the U.S. Information Technology Trade Mission to Asia in Hong Kong, Taiwan, and Korea in June 2000. The Trade Mission featured nine leading U.S.

firms in various technology sectors and was coordinated around the World Congress on Information Technology in Taipei, Taiwan, also in June 2000.

One participating company, Digital Bridge, Inc., is a global E-business builder. The company designs, develops, and delivers strategy-based E-business enterprise solutions. Services are designed to improve a client company's competitive position within its market, through Digital Bridge's expertise in strategic planning, creative design and corporate brand development, technical architecture and complex information systems.

The Asia Trade Mission provided a platform for Digital Bridge to demonstrate how its IT services and Bridge Engine Suite of products can assist Asian/Pacific companies with their critical IT issues with global impact.

Jeffrey Liew, vice president of Asia/Pacific Business Development, stated: "With the United States lowering the barrier to do business in China and the recent announcement of ChinaReform.com selecting Digital Bridge as its IT Partner, this is a perfect opportunity for us to pursue further opportunities in Asia."[13]

Digital Bridge's IT solutions and products catapult its Asia/Pacific and other global client companies into the Internet and E-business marketplace. Digital Bridge's focus is to provide emerging and existing businesses with a rapid and cost effective method for constructing a fully integrated technology platform. This enables any organization preparing for E-business to stay ahead of the technology curve and concentrate on its core business.

Many who follow the Asian economy expect on-line E-commerce sales in Asia to surge, from $2 billion in 1999 to $32.6 billion in 2003, with substantial growth in Taiwan, among the fastest countries to adapt to E-commerce.

For example, the board of Aaeon Technology, a Taiwan maker of specialty computers, typical of the thousands of small companies that make Asia the world's workshop, spent $500,000 for a software system that would enable it to manage parts procurement, inventory, sales, and finances over the Web. It was a huge leap for Aaeon, but the company figured it had no choice. Jessica Chu, Aaeon's marketing manager, was quoted in *Business Week* as saying, "If we want to stay competitive, we need to have E-commerce."[14]

It's hard to believe, as of this writing, that the Internet is already in its fourth decade, although wide consumer use is less than 20 years. As exciting and promising as it seems today, we still haven't really begun to realize its enormous potential, or make full use of its great freedom of movement. In effect, we're still in the Internet's Stone Age.

How the Internet will further evolve is hard to predict. What influence and power will it wield over lifestyles to come? Over businesses? Over customers? Can we establish appropriate new mind-sets to make full use of it? What other marvels of technology will the Internet lead us to?

You can count on one thing: the E-customer is here for good. And his or her special communications vehicle, the Internet, is bound to play an extraordinarily unique and critical role in all the various aspects of future globalization and global branding efforts.

Ten Key Points to Review and Remember

1. The Internet is changing how companies compete, how they approach the global marketplace. Customer wants, needs, opinions, and beliefs cross borders and change cultures with speed and power.

2. Your website is a reflection of everything the brand and company represent. It's where everything comes together, including products and services, customer support, overall attitude, and voice.

3. The Internet, in addition to building new brands and embellishing the established, is also the obvious means of introducing companies to E-business and thus lowering prices, adding customers, and boosting productivity.

4. Like the town square marketplace of long ago, electronic exchanges bring together buyers and sellers. Already hundreds of business-to-business websites make markets in particular fields, linking buyers with sellers and integrating sourcing, purchasing, and billing for all involved parties.

5. Brand involvement on the Web builds brand relationships, which in turn drive long-term loyalty, which is ultimately the driver of business profitability. Four ways to help build customer brand involvement:

- Seek ways to provide helpful services or information that reinforce the brand's proposition.
- Incorporate feedback loops so consumers can comment on the website.
- Try to personalize the site rather than just customize it.
- Deliver on promises in order to build trust.

6. Three approaches to the creation and promotion of on-line brands:

- Create an entirely new brand, unencumbered by any past negative history.
- Employ the name of the off-line parent company for the new on-line brand.
- Create a new brand but make its connection to the more familiar parent known.

7. There are two types of brand: one that conveys facts or beliefs about product attributes, and one that communicates an experience with the product, including feelings, associations, and/or memories.

8. The move from wired telecommunications to wireless is particularly significant to the process of crossing borders. For example, the "third generation" of digital phones makes it possible to access the Internet at lightning speed.

9. If the wired revolution changed the way we think about distance, the wireless revolution changes the way we think about place—it allows you to "take your world with you," to take the latest tools of communication into areas where traditional phone companies cannot reach.

10. Enthusiasm for the Internet isn't limited to North American and European companies. It is also engulfing Asia, a portent of a substantial growth in E-business to come, with B2B already its fastest growing area.

7

Communicating the Brand in an Interactive World

THE IMPORTANCE OF brands keeps growing apace in the United States, as well as all over the world. Faced with a confusing array of competing offerings and marketing messages, consumers and business customers alike rely increasingly on brands to guide their buying choices, and this is perhaps especially so in the interactive markets of the Internet.

The sophisticated communication skills required to advance the brand and the corporate vision in the home marketplace become even more vital in the global marketplace where cultures, values, languages, and traditions can change so drastically when borders are crossed.

Considering the value of clear, continuing communications, I can only agree with Paul Temporal when he writes:

> A total communications strategy is of critical importance to brand build-
> ing, as it determines the effectiveness of image creation. Communica-
> tion delivers the promise of the brand that consumers will experience.
> The tone and style of communications reflect the brand personality, and
> the choice of media impacts the segment penetration.
>
> Communications practices are changing rapidly. . . . As markets
> become more fragmented, audiences more sophisticated, and tech-

121

nologies develop so quickly, the opportunities to communicate with consumers about a brand become almost endless. Linked to this is increasing evidence suggesting that traditional advertising messages do not work anywhere close to the effectiveness with which they used to. . . .

One has to be careful with the use of advertising in its traditional forms, and should put together an integrated communications plan that makes use of a variety of ways by which to bring the brand to people's attention.[1]

Ten-Step Strategy

Best Practices in Corporate Communications (BPCC), a division of the Public Affairs Group, a public relations and strategic communications firm, studies reports on the philosophies, tactics, and initiatives of companies whose business success can be attributed to either a specific aspect of corporate communications or to an efficient and effective communications strategy in general. It has found the following 10-step strategy for global communications especially effective:

1. **Communication efforts match the business plan** at the global, regional, and country levels.

2. **Staffing is critical, a global mix is best, and global training is essential.** Companies are appointing experienced staff to the international public relations and public affairs functions both at headquarters and in the field. Overseas staff generally includes a mix of U.S. citizens and employees from the host country. Best Practices companies provide global training for headquarters and field staff.

3. **Innovative internal communications** between all corporate levels: In-Country, Regional, and Global. It is imperative to maintain a consistent flow of communications between corporate headquarters and field offices.

4. **Mix of communications media,** using the most effective mix of print and electronic, both written and verbal, and experimenting with new approaches and measuring results. Personal media relationships prove valuable internationally.

5. **Use of technology** as never before, with both the internal and external use of electronic communications. Use of website is essential to success in global communications.

6. **Combination of promotional areas:** maximizing the mix of communications, marketing, and advertising.

7. **Marketing focus:** marketing becomes more essential as measuring for new customers is part of growth.

8. **Brand communications:** building brand recognition both internationally and country by country.

9. **Government relations, community relations, and media relations** are all critically important when companies go global. In addition to understanding the laws and government structure of the countries where they operate, global companies must understand the culture and operating practices within the country. Conversely, a company must also ensure that its operations and goals are understood by the government officials, in-country media, and international partners and customers. Media relations efforts should include use of some in-country professionals.

10. **Measurement programs:** evaluation programs should include measurement of results at the country and regional levels. Setting up the right measurement programs is very important. Internal measurement is also important.

An Investment in Brand Communications

Reuters has long had a reputation for excellence, for being an accurate and reliable global source for news and financial information. In this new century, it should continue to stand for such qualities as integrity and innovation. Research among its core customer base shows that the Reuters brand is currently very strong in every part of the world except for the United States, where market penetration has been less.

Reuters' corporate identity and brand advertising manager, Eve Zaeschmar, writes:

> As no market is static, and news and financial information are no different, we [have] started to invest in brand communications. The program to revitalize the Reuters brand began . . . with the introduction of a modern corporate identity. [Then we extended our] communications program to include a brand advertising campaign and increased public relations and direct marketing initiatives. . . .
>
> Executive Director Jean-Claude Marchand, responsible for developing Reuters' brand, [has] said: "We need to make more of the great underlying value of our brand. There are many ways we can do this, but a major advertising campaign is one of the best ways to make a significant impact quickly on a large audience."
>
> . . . The objective of the global advertising campaign is to improve market awareness and understanding of our brand. To assess this, we are conducting regular surveys to measure brand recall. . . . In addition we are carrying out a qualitative survey to test whether our advertising is being understood in the way we intended.[2]

MasterCard's Jonathon Gould, senior vice president, writes that his company believes very strongly in a globally consistent brand and branding message, and that this is evidenced by their award-winning "Priceless" advertising campaign, currently running in 45 countries worldwide.

In addition, MasterCard maintains a consistent and constant presence at the point-of-sale with strong product iconology. The MasterCard logo and interlocking circles are not translated or compromised in any way, providing consumers with the assurance that they have use of a consistent product globally.

The value of advertising in advancing the brand is neatly reaffirmed by Shelly Lazarus, chairman and CEO of Ogilvy Worldwide. In a recent speech, she quoted David Ogilvy as having said: "Every advertisement is part of the long-term investment in the personality of the brand."

An Interactive Medium

There is little doubt that the most exciting, provocative communications tool in today's high-tech world is the Internet. Whereas television audiences have been steadily falling off, the popularity of the Web is increasing exponentially. Advertising spending on the Internet is estimated to rise from $3.3 billion in 1999 to $33 billion by 2004, with perhaps a third of this to be spent outside North America, as compared with 15 percent today. Three years from now as many as 250 million people may well be on-line around the world.

The World Wide Web has attained a high level of achievement as an advertising medium far faster than either television or radio did. Although many companies have awakened to the advertising value of the Web, few fully understand how to make best use of it. Many throw money at the Web in the hope of reaching a mass audience, and so build a brand, just as they used to do in radio and television.

Concurrent with this misunderstanding, many marketers regard on-line advertising much as they see traditional advertising. They pay little notice to the Internet's most telling characteristic: that it is an interactive medium, one that allows both buyer and seller the opportunity to talk directly with one another in real time . . . allows the advertiser to discover the actual interests of the customer and so custom design an offer instantly. On-line advertising has about the same impact as 30-second television commercials, but with this one important extra benefit: the Internet is a much more active medium.

The Web was made for branding. The speed, breadth, depth, and efficiency of the Internet clearly represent the present and the future of business, both in consumer and business-to-business markets. Because the Internet enables companies to manage audience experiences in a more controlled and meaningful way, it has the potential to make brands more relevant and more impactful to customers, resulting in stronger one-to-one relationships and enhanced customer loyalty.

I would be remiss, however, if I did not point out that although surely a valuable medium, the Internet can sometimes present complications. For example, the Internet allows MasterCard to maintain a consistent message in one more—and certainly important—medium. Their challenge is to encourage the vast number of sites that accept Master-Card to use the brand mark and its representations properly. The problem is, with so many new sites daily, monitoring them efficiently is difficult.

Today's Internet customers have access to more information, making them more aware of and more sophisticated about many things—not the least, business issues. A range of choices—one that no real-world shopping mall can match—is available instantly, any day, at any hour. With minimal costs of entry, companies large and small are providing these customers with an ever-expanding number of alternatives, making competition increasingly intense and only a click away. We better get used to it: on the Internet, the customer calls the shots.

Just how interactive the Web can be is plainly demonstrated by Nike's Nike iD project and its offer to sell customized sneakers directly to the consumer through its website. It is the first major shoemaker to do so. For less than $100, shoppers can design their own pair of sneakers by selecting the color, size, and even a nickname to imprint on the heel and then see a mock-up version of their custom sneaks on screen. Once the order is placed, a confirmation E-mail promises delivery of the shoes within three weeks. A few weeks later, another E-mail from Nike alerts the buyer that his or her shoes have been manufactured and sent via second-day shipping free of charge. Nike's attention to detail continues on all the way down to the packaging and the final contents. An unusual cylindrical cardboard container arrives on the buyer's doorstep housing not only the sneakers but also a Nike iD T-shirt featuring the buyer's name silk-screened on the sleeve, a custom "blueprint" of the shoes, and a metal Nike iD dog tag. These additional customized freebies are an added surprise for the consumer.

As you might imagine, the Nike iD project is aimed at getting close to the consumer before competition does. As the project evolves, all individual customers' shoe designs created and sold on-line will be stored in a Web database. The customer will thus be able to order the same shoes as before, and even make minor alterations. The information in this database will also have important impact on those shoes Nike massmanufactures for the retail trade.

The future of the Internet as a marketing resource is mind-boggling, yet many marketers are not taking full advantage of its great potential.

For instance, the Internet can be used to tell if an advertisement is effective, and companies can determine whether they are aiming the right messages at the right people. The combination of interaction and precision marketing makes the Internet an ideal selling tool.

Internet advertisers use a number of techniques, including banners, buttons, interstitials, and superstitials. Even E-mail. But novelty on the Web can be imitated easily and can soon wear off, so most marketers

A VISION OF INTERNET FUTURE

Hewlett-Packard CEO Carly Fiorina outlined the company's vision of a new era in which the promise and reality of the Internet will serve every need, from mundane household tasks to the demands of a fully connected society.

Fiorina called HP's new E-speak software technology fundamental to the brokering of services on the Internet, and said that the end of the product era is approaching, to be replaced by a new era of high technology that will connect services and appliances in an infrastructure. HP is focused, the CEO explained, on "the intersection" where services, appliances, and infrastructure meet.

Companies are looking for anything in the "on-Net" process because service drives customers' experiences and generates profits. "Real success will marry the best of the old bricks-and-mortar world to the dot-coms, the old guard to the new turks," Fiorina said. HP is now in discussions with other companies on ways to deliver Internet appliances and services to the marketplace.

Fiorina also announced a $200 million global brand campaign featuring the company's HP logo, underscored by *invent.* "Our new brand will give us a clearer, stronger voice in the marketplace, and the world will get a picture of us that reflects our true inventiveness," she said.[3]

will continue to rely on off-line media to build their brands. Those who think the Web is for building brands are only kidding themselves. New brands need to be promoted where most of the people are: off-line.

Whether off-line or on-line, it's just as important to communicate clearly and consistently with your own employees as it is with your customers. Employee support of the global brand as well as their understanding of company vision, values, and direction are prerequisites to corporate success—Oshkosh B'Gosh is a good example.

DOUGLAS HYDE, FROM DOMESTIC PRODUCER TO GLOBAL MARKETER

From the author's interview with Douglas Hyde, president and CEO of Oshkosh B'Gosh, Inc.

When I took over as president and CEO, our communications were very hierarchical—as was probably the case in many companies. The previous CEO—who was my father—ran the company very differently. There wasn't a lot of communication; it was kind of on a "need to know" basis. Often there were broad constituencies that he felt didn't need to know a lot. And I think that was fairly typical of that generation and how they managed communications in their companies.

When we started going through a significant transformation in 1992 and '93, we obviously felt a lot differently in general about communications. Considering the amount of change that was before us, we believed it was important to communicate more often, in greater detail, and with a degree of frequency that really wasn't in existence in the past.

Our company needed to go through a fairly major transformation from a domestic producer of product to a global marketing company. Along with this transformation, a lot of domestic plants were closed, with a lot of layoffs and restructuring changes. We needed to make sure that people understood why we were doing it and what our company goals were. It was really this that made us recognize the need for communication, more so than in the past when the thinking was more "status quo."

Now, working with our HR department, we hold "state of the corporation" meetings quarterly. These meetings include about 70 vice presidents, directors, and managers. At each meeting there is a brief period at the beginning when we talk about the current quarterly financials and we go through the line business by business to see how we're tracking against plan.

Then we have some of our other executives give reports on how their specific businesses are going. Maybe we start with a retail presentation, where we'll have one quarter in wholesale, another in licensing, etc. So there's a little more in depth. What we're really dealing with here are future plans as opposed to a history of the past quarter. The attempt is to give the people who are in charge of making things happen a sense of being in the loop and understanding what's going on.

Strategy Review

There is always a talk about the strategy itself. In 1995 we went through a major strategic planning initiative, and, obviously, the outcome of that needed to be communicated. Which we did. And at every meeting after the quarterly review I talk about the strategy and put out the same strategic initiatives, in the same format, time after time after time. I do this on purpose, so people know that the strategy hasn't changed. It's the same as last quarter and as last year. It is kind of how we track on those initiatives.

Vice presidents, directors, and managers are expected to communicate the strategy themselves down to their own people. We found when we first started doing this that some were very good at those communications and others were not. It was somewhat inconsistent. So now we have a formal piece that comes out within 10 days of those state-of-the-corporation meetings—a piece that articulates and tries to encapsulate the content of the meeting's discussion as a handout to the broader cross section of employees.

As far as those directors and managers who do not communicate well are concerned, we do not attempt to teach them better communication techniques. Some of our HR people have had conversations with them, but frankly, we've resigned ourselves to the fact that we have a fairly broad spectrum of communication skills. It's not that we don't want to encourage them to improve, but we know full well that some are going to do it better than others.

That's why we instituted the quarterly document. It assures that the basis of what is discussed at each meeting is placed in

continued

everyone's hand. Each manager elaborates on that to varying degrees.

In-Country Partners

We are, of course, a global company. The vast majority of our global business, however, is not done with owned and operated subsidiaries or divisions. It's licensed. In-country partners—who in and of themselves are business people running their own businesses—produce our lines of apparel. This is growing in importance, and we look to further growth in the future. Communications are a little different globally because the relationships are different and our partners are different. But it certainly is now at a much higher level than it has been previously.

We communicate with them about our marketing and advertising plans for the coming year. From a product standpoint, they're very looped in. They look at what we're doing here in the States and modify it to the extent necessary for applicability in their home markets.

Typically in our international meetings—there are two a year—I give a little overview, but at an even higher level, of how we're doing as a company. Naturally they, as licensees, are very concerned with how well we're doing here in the States. It gives them a comfort level to know we're still doing well. We talk about share information and the market research we have. They really get a good feeling for what's happening to our business here, and it's possible to impact on what they're doing in their countries.

I am personally involved in advertising decisions, and describe myself as Global Brand Manager. Product development, advertising, and marketing all report to me, and I think I have a good sense of it. I should—I've been doing it for 20-some-odd years now. I make sure that the brand is communicated the way it needs to be, and that it's done consistently around the world.

Often it's a challenge, especially when you're dealing with 40 or 50 licensees who all, to some degree, want to interpret what Oshkosh is in order to make it more appropriate in their view for their home markets. We've done a lot of work to minimize that, and only do it to a small degree where necessary. So we begin to build consistency in how the brand is communicated. Whether it's the product advertising, how it's marketed, what retail stores look like, or whatever, it seems to work.

GLOBAL BRAND CONTROL

Royal Dutch/Shell does business in more than 100 countries and at more than 40,000 retail sites. Simon Saville is the manager of Global Brand Standards for the company, and it's his job to be sure Shell's familiar seashell logo looks just right on every business card, letterhead, advertisement, gas station sign, and so forth.

"The brand is not just a pretty design or a logo," he says. "It is what we believe in, what our customers can expect when they see the Shell logo—the symbol of the brand. The brand is the thing that binds us together, sets Shell apart from its competitors, makes people choose, trust, and believe in us."[4]

Keeping watch over that brand is not an easy job, considering the number of offices to be checked worldwide. But all that is changing. Shell is beginning to use the Internet to control corporate brand governance. Writes John Evan Frook: "As part of a program called One Brand, Shell has replaced visual identity manuals with a website that is updated regularly. . . . It also plans to use the site for management of cooperative advertising programs and shared creative materials."[5]

The Shell brand was valued recently by trade publications at $2.9 billion, considerably less than the $5 billion senior management believed. In response to this apparent erosion of Shell's brand integrity, the One Brand companywide initiative was

continued

launched. Says Saville: "By not adequately controlling brand image, we were allowing differences to be perpetuated."[6] The aim of One Brand is to align external perceptions by consistently communicating the corporate brand and thus make clear to customers what Shell stands for.

Shell is by no means alone in using the Internet to control its global brand. According to Frook:

> Erich Joachimsthaler says corporate branding is in the midst of a revolution. IBM and Cisco Systems have spurred it, using the Web to protect and build their brands. Both have been effective in using the Internet as a platform for their entire marketing communications. Now, other companies are headed down the same path. . . .
>
> Shell has seen its One Brand site grow at warp speed. . . . So far, the site has been used to update regularly the way the brand is treated globally. Additional services are being rolled out, including distribution of creative advertising materials suited for multiple markets and a cooperative advertising area for planning partnerships and budgets. . . . Shell [also plans to] introduce distribution of TV ads on the site.[7]

That Shell's global brand is growing in power is evident by recent ratings of oil company brands. In 1999 Shell moved up to number seven among U.S. oil brands in the Corporate Branding Power Ratings study, having missed out on the top ten altogether in 1998.

These ratings measure how familiar and favorable a brand is to 400 key business decision makers, defined as VPs or higher at the top 20 percent of U.S. corporations based on revenue.

Defining Core Values

One global company that believes strongly in the value of communications in today's high-tech world is the National Australia Bank Group. One of Australia's outstanding corporate successes during the past decade or so, its core values have been key in managing growth. In fact, they represent a major aspect of the philosophy that supports the company vision of building a world-class, global network of integrated financial service organizations.

Don Argus, Group Managing Director and CEO, explains: "We found ourselves in a situation where the pervasive changes taking place in the industry were escalating the need to make our own internal organizational changes."

Having surveyed those within the company, "we gained critical insights . . . Through a combination of one-on-one interviews, focus groups, and a quantitative survey involving over 900 managers . . . [we gained] the base of information we needed to create the new values-driven organization."[8]

Understanding that values are the core beliefs and habits of any organization, Argus and his management team recognized that they had to be relevant to the business and accepted by employees. The result was the development of seven basic core values:

- Service to customers
- Quality in everything
- Professionalism and ethics in all actions
- Competitiveness and a will to win
- Growth and development of all employees
- Continuous improvement in productivity
- Growing profit for stakeholders

Communicating Core Values

Having defined the company's core values, Argus and his team set about communicating them throughout the company, clearly and effectively. Since it was important for National's people to live these values fully, a major communications and training program was instituted to inform, involve, and motivate the employees.

Additional programs were introduced for the managers. With more than 40 percent of National's asset base outside its home country, its global business reach added still another dimension to the development, communication, and employment of values.

As National developed into a global business, it was clear that its traditional local bankers' way of managing was not going to work in the future. Change was required for continuing success, but major shifts in corporate values don't happen automatically. Defining, communicating, and propagating its core values would have to be a continuing process, and to be truly effective, it would have to be instilled at all levels and in all locales of the organization.

Argus explains: "While [core] values provide a strong foundation for a business, they can be difficult to communicate and even harder to implement. To meet this challenge, we developed a number of highly innovative communications programs, ranging from the traditional group video and publications and presentations, to business television and strategic mapping. It wasn't easy . . . nevertheless, the seven core values are becoming pervasive throughout the business and deeply influencing the way daily activities are conducted."[9]

Sharing Strategic Vision

Today, most multinational companies are moving full speed ahead on an obstacle course. The truth is, global companies can't slow down. Competitors are too close, too fast, too eager to take risks. Today's volatile business environment requires management to be nimble in responding to fast-changing market dynamics. So reducing speed is not an option. We can, however, prepare our companies to respond quickly when danger—or opportunity—crosses our path.

We need to make sure our people and processes are ready for sudden change. In short, we need very fast and reliable lines of communication. And the one thing we need to communicate clearly and consistently, throughout our organizations, is strategic vision. Too often top managers neglect to spend the needed time and effort to fully inform and educate employees on company vision. Too often strategic vision is thought of as some musty, leather-bound volume sitting on a bookshelf and reserved only for special occasions.

We don't make it widely accessible and therefore it doesn't become a living, breathing part of every day's business activities. Or else we offer it as some sort of propaganda that doesn't square with the reality of how we actually do business every day.

Despite all the communications channels available—including such impressive new technologies as intranets—the connection between a company's strategic vision and its ground-level activities often remains vague and confused in the minds of managers and employees alike. The message of the vision may not even be taken seriously.

How can you be sure your vision is coming through loud and clear? That it is fully understood and accepted? By listening very, very carefully—to managers and employees alike. Measure the performance of your managers especially on a great deal more than productivity and reliability.

At least one major corporation I know of has developed a "balanced scorecard" assessment system that examines how well each manager understands and promotes the objectives and strategies of the company. This system, invented at Harvard, also aligns compensation and promotion with each manager's handling of such issues as quality, people skills, costs, and business development.

Be sure to keep communications always focused on the finish line and aligned with your strategic vision. Work to get managers and employees to think of global operations as more than a mere adjunct to domestic business. Strive to get them to make the leap from saying "We have global operations" to thinking "We are a global company." Ingrain the global mind-set in everything you do to achieve your strategic vision. This should always be a top communications priority.

The Personal Approach

Global branding, like corporate branding, encompasses all of a company's planned communications. The individual techniques of communication and their emphasis vary from company to company and from CEO to CEO, with the CEO's own abilities and style bearing as heavily on the use of specific communication methods as on the creation and maintenance of the brand.

In reaching company managers, employees, and key shareholders, the more personal approach of face-to-face conversations and/or handwritten notes is currently favored by many CEOs. It should be no surprise that in today's high-tech world E-mail and voice mail are also increasingly the standard.

Jac Nasser, president and CEO of Ford Motor Co., is one leader who believes strongly in personal employee communication. As Ford's Automotive Operations president, he held weekly group meetings in which he taught employees—a total of 50,000 to date—about shareholder value, price/earnings ratios, and other business fundamentals.

He's done this in lecture halls, offices, and factories around the world, spending hours with the crowds, poring over flip charts and taking questions from the floor.

Sue Zesigner, wrote about it for *Fortune*:

> Each Friday afternoon, he drafts and sends out a "personal" E-mail to 89,000 Ford employees worldwide. . . . Within each note—often several screens long—Nasser shares the highlights and insights of his week, good news, bad news, and the occasional employee challenge. It's easy to imagine that employees . . . feel immediately a part of the inner circle. . . . The just-between-you-and-me tone is striking.
>
> Hundreds of workers from around the world respond to his E-mails every month; Nasser reads each one and assigns a member of his team to answer it personally. . . . Nasser's best skill is his ability to make every person he interacts with feel important.[10]

Repeat the Message

Few have personified successful corporate leadership more notably than Jack Welch, CEO of General Electric. Most great leaders are masters at communicating their desires. In his early years as chief executive, Welch discovered that you can't merely dictate change; nor can you simply communicate with only people at the top levels and expect changes to occur. So Welch keeps repeating key messages and reinforcing them at every turn.

The gist of Welch's key messages distill his vision for GE: that it be number one or number two in every one of its businesses. That his employees get the message is evident. Led by Welch, they have advanced the brand and taken the company to almost unprecedented prosperity. Currently, GE boasts more than $300 billion in assets and $90 billion in sales, with 276,000 employees in more than 100 countries.

How does Welch command so much influence and power over such a large, global organization? Basically, through sheer force of personality, impelled by an irrepressible passion for winning. Above all, he's an unwavering believer in the power of his people, and he makes it his business to get to know them, always keeping lines of communication open.

Welch's strength is his mastery of the principles of motivation. He writes notes to managers and employees, suggesting changes, thanking them, making note of family crises. He also teaches at GE's training center, lecturing his managers, cajoling them, listening to them. His brash candor defines GE's corporate culture.

He knows his people, how best to guide them, and their significance to the brand. He also understands the value of surprise, and every week there are drop-in visits to plants and offices, hurriedly scheduled luncheons with managers several layers below him, and countless handwritten notes to GE employees.

Rarely does Welch miss the opportunity to make his presence felt. His personal notes are sent to everyone from top executives to hourly workers. They carry enormous impact because they are intimate and spontaneous, written to inspire and motivate as much as to demand action. All of this does much to influence constructively the behavior of a vast and complex organization and support its role in building and maintaining the global brand.

Consultation and Consensus

Like GE, companies that are serious about promoting their brands globally understand the need for communication and cooperation between headquarters and their many facilities, subsidiaries, and partners around the world. Research on managing the corporate brand confirms this, indicating that although patterns of organization among firms with experience in global branding are diverse, whatever their structure, all stress the need for consultation and consensus-building between the corporate office and local or regional personnel.

From the same study, Jamie Murray of DuPont says:

Our management role is collaborative. Our global team for brand management links together members of the management committee from key regions such as North America, Europe, and Asia. They meet quarterly, and have frequent teleconferences in between.

We work with data drawn from worldwide opinion surveys to determine DuPont's greatest needs, whether opportunities or remedial actions. Recommendations and implementation are done on a consultative basis with country management. We reconcile the global team's positions with the needs of the businesses.[11]

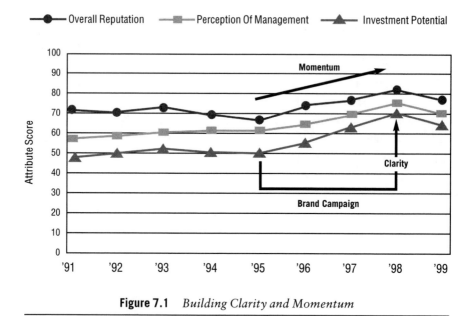

Figure 7.1 *Building Clarity and Momentum*

I am frequently asked the question: "How do you translate a corporate message to global markets?" As always, my response is: with caution, great caution. It is a rare campaign that can run globally without adjustments in various local markets. It makes sense, therefore, to understand the markets around the world on a country-by-country basis.

This analysis will help companies measure the clarity of the message and the momentum of a corporate campaign. Clarity and momentum are two essential measures of successful branding. If the campaign isn't working, this can be determined quickly and the advertising changed appropriately.

Keep in mind that even if a corporation has many divisions, subsidiaries, and affiliates, it is not the role of a corporate/global branding campaign to replace product or divisional brand campaigns. Rather, the purpose is to help key audiences understand the parent company and its vision for the future. It may not always be appropriate for the corporation to be visible to consumers of the company's products, but it nearly always makes sense for the parent company to be visible to other key constituencies, such as shareholders, employees, government officials, vendors, etc.

Ten Key Points to Review and Remember

1. Communications practices are changing rapidly as markets become more fragmented, audiences more sophisticated, and technologies develop so quickly.

2. Ten-step strategy for global communications:
   - Communication efforts match business plan
   - Global staffing
   - Innovative internal communications
   - Effective mix of media
   - Use of technology, with website essential
   - Combination of promotional areas
   - Marketing focus
   - Brand communication
   - Government, community, and media relations
   - Right measurement programs

3. Every advertisement is part of the long-term investment in the personality of the brand.

4. The Internet is an interactive medium, one that allows both buyer and seller the opportunity to talk directly with one another in real time, allowing the advertiser to discover the actual interests of the customer and so custom design an offer instantly.

5. To better control brand image, a major oil producer replaced heavy visual identity manuals with a website that is updated regularly . . . and it plans to use the site also for the management of cooperative advertising programs and the sharing of creative materials.

6. One large overseas financial institution, in determining its values and core beliefs, has developed seven basic core values which are pertinent to most organizations:
   - Service to customers
   - Quality in everything
   - Professionalism and ethics in all actions
   - Competitiveness and a will to win
   - Growth and development of all employees
   - Continuous improvement in productivity
   - Growing profit for stakeholders

7. One of the biggest challenges confronting corporations today is the process of communicating strategic vision throughout their organizations. If the vision isn't made widely accessible, it won't become a living part of every day's business activities.

8. Two potential traps in getting the message to the front lines are: (1) taking for granted that middle management is on board, and (2) senior management hasn't made the message both convincing and compelling to the rest of the corporation.

9. There is no technology or communications channel more powerful or effective in sharing information than face-to-face interaction.

10. Understand your markets around the world on a country-by-country basis. It is a rare campaign that can run globally without making some local adjustments.

8

Merging the Brands

THE 1990S WITNESSED an astonishing number of mergers and acquisitions, with $1.7 trillion worth of deals announced in 1999 alone. The United Nations reports that the dollar value of cross-border mergers and acquisitions grew from $85 billion in 1991 to $850 billion in 1999. And merger activity is still frantic, with hundreds initiated each week, many taking corporate participants a long way toward globalization.

Mergers of corporations also mean the mergers of corporate brands. Sometimes the result is a new brand, such as DaimlerChrysler or Verizon, this latter the result of merging Bell Atlantic with GTE. Often one of the brands is wiped out. The merger of BP Petroleum and Amoco leaves only BP as an active brand. And when Chase Manhattan and Chemical banks merged, only the Chase name and brand survived.

Actually, mergers can prove hazardous. Fewer than half the mergers completed during the '80s and '90s created real value for shareholders. Consulting firm McKinsey & Co. claims that nearly 80 percent of mergers do not earn back the costs of the deals themselves. Moreover, *Across the Board* says the average merger has a 50 percent chance of achieving reduced productivity and/or profits.

Mergers, and the talk surrounding them, can hurt stock prices also. When rumors of a takeover bid for Chevron by the Royal Dutch/Shell Group withered, Chevron stock declined. Similarly, Consolidated Freightways Corp. stock fell as much as 18 percent after it broke off its own merger talks, only to rise 6.4 percent on speculation of another possible combination.

Then, too, mergers typically engender confusion, conflict, fear, anger, and uncertainty among employees. This can lead to talent raiding—nonmerging companies scooping up good people who are worried about their futures just when distracted executives need them most. Not a very pretty picture.

What's the problem? What is it that makes the difference? The integration process—or rather, the lack of one—has by and large been blamed for merger failure.

Cross-Culture Integration

Gianpaolo Caccini, president and chief executive of Saint-Gobain Corporation, notes that the usual cultural differences between companies intensify when the companies are located in different countries. Americans, for example, tend to be direct, which can seem combative, even insulting, to Europeans. In contrast, a European's softer approach can frustrate Americans, who feel as if they're not getting their message across.

Caccini goes on to observe:

> Eastern practices also differ dramatically. In China, things seem to take a long time. The Chinese don't yet believe, as Westerners do, that time is money. . . .
>
> Especially with large international acquisitions, a cultural assessment should be as much a part of due diligence as legal and financial issues. If you decide to go ahead with the merger, you'll at least be prepared for the complexities involved to succeed. Cross-culture integration can be done successfully, but it takes a long time, careful planning, and lots of patience. . . .
>
> The integration will take longer than you planned, cost more than you expect, and cause more stress in both organizations that you can imagine. My main advice is to be flexible and stay focused on your objectives.[1]

"Merger of Equals"

In 1994 General Re Corporation, the leading reinsurer in North America, acquired Cologne Re, which, although not as large, was the oldest reinsurance company in the world, with a network of international offices. General Re, looking to become a global company, determined that it would be easier, faster, more efficient and cost effective to acquire a company that could provide an immediate global network—as opposed to opening their own individual offices.

The acquisition was conducted in a spirit of cooperation and agreement, as if in a merger of equals. From the beginning the two companies demonstrated much cooperation and collaboration. For example, they created councils—such as Finance, New Products, HR, and Underwriting—that worked closely on issues in their areas. In general, however, each company continued to operate as it had, on its own, for some time after the acquisition.

As a result, the two companies actually joined together quite slowly in order to build trust, respect, and commitment. Although now operating a single, global corporation, they continued to function autonomously in their respective markets and under their old names.

Although this was now a global company with global resources, it was not yet integrated—either from a branding standpoint or from an operational one. However, they did globalize three large units very quickly: Global Casualty Facultative, Global Property Facultative, and the Multi National Business Unit. But reinsurance is very much a relationship business, based on long-term professional and personal associations. These are founded on trust and respect, and neither company wanted to disturb those relationships.

Eventually, however, a new trade name was adopted for all of the smaller international markets that had once been part of Cologne Re. The new name was General & Cologne Re, and legal entities in those markets were changed to this. In Germany, however, Cologne Re's biggest market, the company continued to operate under its old name. General Re also kept its name in North America. But the rest of the world used General & Cologne Re, and there was also some sort of tactical ad hoc usage of this trade name in both North America and Germany.

So, essentially, there were three brands in the global marketplace, all kind of equal and coexisting, with no particular guidelines. There were also, of course, two different business philosophies, two different cultures—in fact, two different business models.

Cologne Re, a relatively small company compared to big globals like Swiss Re and Munich Re, was generally relegated to a position as a third choice provider. Most German companies would never give all their business to one company anyway; they would split it up into a diversified portfolio. Cologne Re's objective was to be a strong alternative to Munich Re and Swiss Re, which as a practical matter meant being in the third position. This philosophy was in direct opposition to the General Re culture—which was and is to seek ways to win 100 percent of the business whenever possible.

For the most part the two companies cooperated but operated on their own tracks. So the new global corporation functioned with two different IT departments, two different accounting systems, two management structures—two of everything, and everything separate.

It didn't take long for General Re and Cologne Re to realize that at some point they were going to have to integrate. With competition keen and aggressive in a soft market, the company knew it must do everything possible to improve marketplace position.

Among key measures to be taken were the building of a single solid global brand and the improvement of operating efficiencies. This meant the company had to rapidly integrate on a global basis, and thus reduce redundancies.

At this writing, the company has just gone through its global reorganization. Management structure has been changed and has established six different operating regions to streamline the company and improve its capability to service clients better and manage risks better. All this is happening concurrently with the rolling out of a new, global branding strategy.

One of the biggest concerns with the reorganization was that Germans and other Europeans in the company might have to become more like Americans and adopt an American work style. So it was crucial to be extra careful to celebrate the diversity in their organization, to reassure everyone that one of the company's great and unique strengths is the power of its cultural differences and that it continues to leverage this power effectively.

Both General Re and Cologne Re, unlike many of their competitors, have always tried to manage their international offices with local nationals. Today there is some commingling in terms of senior management, but there is not much general cross-pollination—not surprising because this is a business driven by relationships, and clients generally prefer to work with people of a common nationality.

Many but not all clients are relatively small, regional insurance companies. Because they are not global, they don't really care about global capacity or resources. They just want to work with someone who understands the issues they face. There's nothing wrong with being big and global—it's good to know they can share resources and intelligence on a global basis—but you still have to be locally minded. In other words, be global but think local.

A key part of the integration process was the origination of a company branding strategy with its promise focused primarily on underwriting and the integrity of the company—both important core values. Thus, the new brand personality reflects the kind of client-oriented companies General Re and Cologne Re have always been.

With the strategy established, one of the biggest issues was the creation and implementation of a new brand. The most visible expressions of a brand are, of course, the name and logo. A number of new corporate names were considered, with the final choice being GeneralCologne Re, a symbol of who they are and what their clients can expect from them. The name not only characterizes the strong equity offered by both former brands, but is a clear expression to all the world of the seamless, cohesive way this new, combined company does business. In effect, the new name represents both the rich heritage of the past and the promise of a very bright future. It embodies total dedication to the concept: One Brand. One Company. One Promise.

The company's new logo features a distinctive icon, symbolizing the vision with which GeneralCologne Re approaches business. Styled as a lamp, it is a beacon whose light shines forth into a future of commitment and promise.

In a letter to corporate colleagues, chairman and CEO Ronald E. Ferguson wrote: "Our new structure will allow us to move faster, smarter and more effectively in all our international markets. . . . We are operating in a fast-paced world of interconnectedness, a world of networks with E-commerce taking center stage. Every minute matters. The

Figure 8.1   *Annual Review*

Figure 8.2   *Brand Book*

Clarity of

Our brand grows stronger when we communicate consistently and clearly with one voice. We have four key messages that serve as a foundation for everything we do. Our dedication to these principles distinguishes us from our competitors and guides us on our pathway to future success.

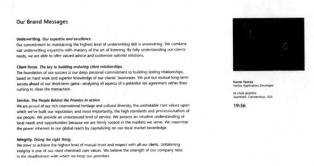

Our Brand Messages

Underwriting. *Our expertise and excellence.*
Our commitment to maintaining the highest level of underwriting skill is unwavering. We combine vast underwriting expertise with mastery of the art of listening. By fully understanding our clients' needs, we are able to offer valued advice and customize optimal solutions.

Client focus. *The key to building enduring client relationships.*
The foundation of our success is our deep personal commitment to building lasting relationships, based on hard work and superior knowledge of our clients' businesses. We put our mutual long-term success ahead of our short-term gains—analyzing all aspects of a potential risk agreement rather than rushing to close the transaction.

Service. *The People Behind the Promise in action.*
We are proud of our rich international heritage and cultural diversity; the unshakable core values upon which we've built our reputation; and most importantly, the high standards and professionalism of our people. We provide an unsurpassed level of service. We possess an intuitive understanding of local needs and opportunities because we are firmly rooted in the markets we serve. We maximize the power inherent in our global reach by capitalizing on our local market knowledge.

Integrity. *Doing the right thing.*
We strive to achieve the highest level of mutual trust and respect with all our clients. Unfaltering integrity is one of our most cherished core values. We believe the strength of our company rests in the steadfastness with which we keep our promises.

Karen Yancey
Senior Application Developer

At choir practice
Stamford, Connecticut, USA

19:56

21

Figure 8.3 *Brand Book*

Courtesy GeneralCologne Re™

time to communicate. The time to connect. The time to listen and understand. Our global network gives us the opportunity to interact with each other even more effectively and bring our knowledge and service to wherever it is needed most."[2]

GeneralCologne Re has started down the road to globalization. The process may seem slow to some, but the care and consideration the two

Figure 8.4 *Financial Review 1999*

Courtesy GeneralCologne Re™

companies have used at the beginning will undoubtedly spell success in the end.

A Manageable Process

Without a well-thought-out integration plan, companies in a merger or acquisition situation may not easily achieve the success desired. BMW, which purchased Rover Group Pic in 1994, found it difficult to turn a profit from the merger. Chairman Bernd Pischetsrieder told *Manager Magazine*: "We made the mistake of not acting quickly enough to push through integrated work processes."

Unless vision and values can be made to align and lines of communication remain open, such processes are doomed. Companies that understand this are more likely to be viewed favorably by potential acquisitions and so experience greater merger success.

For example, the *Wall Street Journal* cites Ford as the automobile industry's "acquirer of choice" given its reputation for "providing capital and expertise without diluting a brand's character." Mergers and acquisitions are here to stay, and business needs to master the necessary skills to execute them successfully. Although most companies view the procedures as onetime events, many are actually involved with a merger or acquisition more than once. But no matter how many times a company may go through it, these can be tension-laden experiences with a loss of jobs, restructured responsibilities, and derailed careers often the result. Little wonder most managers think more about how to get them over with than how to do them better.

Managers should look on acquisition integration as a known, controllable process, not some unique event. One company that does that is GE Capital Services. It has assimilated more than 100 acquisitions and, in the process, has developed a successful model for melding new acquisitions into the corporate structure. A major financial services conglomerate, GE Capital Services operates 27 separate businesses and has more than 50,000 employees worldwide. Nearly half of the company's businesses are located outside the United States, and more than half came from acquisitions.

Consider GE Capital's experience in making acquisitions work on both a financial and organizational basis. GE Capital has learned certain lessons that form a basic framework for the integration of acquisitions, and we would do well to remember them. First, always start integration before the deal is signed, assigning a full-time individual to managing the process. Also, implement any necessary restructuring sooner rather than later. Finally, carefully integrate not only the business operations, but the corporate cultures as well.

Make the Brand Part of the Deal

Acquisition can be a potent strategy for growth and diversification, as Nestlé's more recent history illustrates. Nestlé acquired a multitude of brands, especially in the food and beverage markets, between 1960 and 1990, which called for a consolidation and integration of the company's branding architecture. As a result, Nestlé now fields a number of worldwide corporate brands, including Nestlé, Carnation, and Buitoni. Beyond that, Nestlé markets at least 45 worldwide strategic product brands, 100 regional product brands, and as many as 7,000 local product brands.

Vision, values, and communication are at the heart of brand building, which is contingent on successful brand integration. However, harried executives often slight their corporate or global brands. But since brands rank high among the participating companies' most important assets, they pose key questions at merger time, such as: Which brand should you keep and build on? Should a new brand be introduced?

Because the brand's value is at the heart of integration and is particularly influential during a merger or acquisition, it can—and should—be fiercely protected and put to work immediately on the company's behalf. In fact, making the brand part of the deal is one way to avoid merger breakdown. Get it on the table from the very start.

As I have often stated, the classic corporate brand communicates the company's essence, character, and purpose, and calls to mind its products and services. Correctly created, managed, and presented, the brand—whether corporate or global—should swiftly saturate target audiences with confident and accurate expectations. Why would they want to buy, invest, or work anywhere else?

When a new brand must be created by merging companies, it should purposefully be conceived to shore up confidence and at the same time ignite excitement and action.

Corporate Brand as Lifeline

Research at Corporate Branding indicates that, on average, a corporate brand impacts stock performance by 5 to 7 percent—a significant number that can make a major impression on market valuation.

During turbulent times, particularly in mergers and acquisitions, the corporate brand can be a lifeline. Looking for reassurance that after the merger they will still be able to depend on what they have come to value, all constituencies cling to their corporate brand. It becomes a symbol of future expectations and a reason why the merger is taking place.

Remember, in mergers, all eyes focus on the brand: the media, customers, employees, and investors. The brand provides the kind of visibility that can prove enormously leveragable, so be prepared to exploit this rare communications opportunity. Protect, preserve, and leverage the value of your corporate brand always, but especially during a merger.

The Brand as the Spirit of the Merger

Like it or not, the world will perceive the new brand as symbolic of the rationale underlying the merger. Developing the corporate brand so it reflects your reasoning accurately and appealingly is critical, but only if you ask the same appropriate questions throughout the merger negotiations that one asks in the branding process:

- Why and how does our growth depend on this merger?
- What does it do for us that we could not do on our own?
- What can we expect in the future?
- Will this merger alter our values, mission, and/or vision?
- What do Wall Street, our employees, and our customers expect from us?
- How can we manage these expectations?
- What characteristics and competencies energize our CoreBrand?

Failure to understand and communicate the brand will likely lead to failure of the merger itself. Avoid merger meltdown by defining the essence of your brand from the very beginning—for yourself as well as for your merger partner(s), your employees, your shareholders, and your customers.

Exploit Initial Interest

Your corporate profile is seldom more visible than during the announcement of a merger or acquisition. Be prepared to take full advantage of this remarkable opportunity to communicate on a grand scale. Be especially careful of timing and to adhere to full disclosure rules if you're a publicly traded security.

Keep major decisions absolutely secret until you are ready to announce them, and have a plan in place to deal with news leaks. Think it through thoroughly and then prepare clear, concise, consistent messages to communicate the business logic behind the deal to all audiences, from stakeholders and media to government regulators.

Do not allow a communications vacuum to develop as your merger unfolds. A branding plan, including the corporate name, message, and pertinent materials, should be ready at all times. This is the time to seize the day; your merger will never get more attention than at this moment. Effective, timely corporate communications will influence the opinions of all constituencies. Early communications, just after the announcement, will set the tone, create first impressions (most remembered), and pave the way for overall merger success.

Perhaps the one most important communications tactic is to appoint a senior spokesperson to sow the seeds of your merger's business logic in all the right places—to help your actions become fully understood and appreciated.

An excellent example of the value of early, well-designed communications is seen in the DaimlerChrysler merger, which executed a well-coordinated corporate branding campaign from the outset. Every communication bore the new company's simple, clean, unpretentious name and logo, and was designed specifically to reinforce the underlying logic of the merger.

The senior management of both companies made themselves available to the press, initiating clear and consistent ongoing media relations. DaimlerChrysler's advertising campaign stayed focused on the key issues and spoke vigorously to all constituencies.

No matter how well-coordinated communications programs may be during a merger, however, sometimes companies fail to support the corporate brand sufficiently *after* the merger. Daimler Benz and Chrysler is a case in point. Chrysler had been perceived as a down-market brand, little known to most Europeans, while Mercedes was considered up-market and exclusive. By blurring the distinctiveness of its two major brands, the newly formed company, DaimlerChrysler, risked losing its standing in both markets.

Leverage the Brand

When overanxious executives are intent on just closing the deal, it's problematic to keep an eye on the brand. Still, the intensity of a merger environment offers moments to exhibit your creative brilliance if you actively promote and/or exploit the brand's role in the deal.

It's common in merger announcements, for example, for the big fish to swallow the smaller along with its brand, though this may not always be the best stratagem for long-term brand building. It can pay off nicely to evaluate both existing corporate brands carefully, adopting the one that will work most effectively on behalf of the merged organization and will accurately reflect the companies' combined vision and intent.

Sometimes other considerations force both brands to be subsumed within a totally new one. For instance, postmerger, Ciba-Geigy and Sandoz chose to call themselves Novartis, to indicate the formation of a new, completely different—and integrated—company. Though a sound choice in this case, it's usually realistic to acknowledge the loss of equity that results from walking away from well-established original names and to compensate for the loss.

On the other hand, when the Novartis chemical business was spun off, it called itself Ciba Specialty Chemicals, retaining the old name while adding a descriptor. Though the division was a big brand winner—a well-known entity from day one—the company had to work hard internally to get everyone on the same new team.

Similarly, when companies choose to combine their names in a "read-through," like DaimlerChrysler, there is a tendency to retain divergent cultures if measures are not taken to mesh them into a comfortable new whole. Obviously, there is no one "right" answer, but attending to the brand's role in the deal will guide you toward the right one for you. Remember that any name choice is bound to create its own management and communications issues, which must be carefully resolved.

Merger frenzy in the oil industry offers several examples of effective brand handling—and mishandling. The Royal Dutch/Shell Group bankers jumped the gun several times with premature announcements of pending deals that ultimately misfired. In December 1998 Reuters quoted Chevron Corp.'s chairman and chief executive, Kenneth Derr, who questioned the wisdom of a major merger ". . . if the only thing you are going to get out of it is a one-shot reduction of costs." It's certainly not the compelling reason needed to excite consumers or to start building a strong new brand.

British Petroleum (BP), Amoco, and Atlantic Richfield (ARCO), on the other hand, operating in the same difficult global oil market, were brought together by a series of mergers and acquisitions and negotiated through regulatory hurdles with relative ease. The merger, made between noncompetitors for its good fit, offered a much better opportunity for long-term brand building.

The group, now known as BP, is replacing the familiar BP shield and Amoco torch with a new symbol depicting a sunburst of green, white, and yellow. Called a "Helios mark," the new logo represents dynamic energy. It remains to be seen, however, how customers will react when the familiar Amoco and ARCO brands are dropped in favor of the less familiar BP in the United States.

Create Internal Buy-In

The importance of your own people cannot be exaggerated. A merger can be unnerving for employees, who typically feel apprehensive as they contemplate what it means for the business and for them personally: What will our customers think? Will this work with our current business strategy? What about my job? Do I still have a job? Will I have to relocate? How will I be treated by the new brass?

Sometimes employees need to be coaxed through a merger. Well-planned communications that explain and reinforce brand values can help bring two cultures together more easily and effectively. Reassuring employees, while merging two separate organizations into one, is not an easy task. Carefully thought out and well-executed internal communications, and building a global infrastructure to support the brand over time, can pave the way.

If possible, don't let your employees find out about the merger from the media. Tell them yourself, through a supervisor or a companywide communication, such as a personal announcement from the chairman. And never tell the acquired staff that it will be "business as usual" when you know it won't.

Follow up, early in the game, with a steady stream of communications—newsletters, the company intranet, house organs, paycheck stuffers, bulletin board notices, etc.—explaining merger whys and hows. A few months down the line, pamphlets outlining brand strategy, philosophy, and communication can motivate employees to assimilate the brand and begin to live the brand.

Employee get-togethers, too, can create an esprit de corps between diverse groups. Think about launching a new brand and/or logo with a companywide event. Encourage periodic meetings between groups from each merger partner to identify synergies and to develop processes for working productively together.

Consider establishing a brand council made up of communicators from each part and major location of the company. The council's mission: to ensure clear, consistent brand communications through ongoing development and review, and to create guidelines for universal brand communication.

Avoid the Schizophrenic Brand

Consistency is key to building brand credibility, particularly in global marketing. Be sure to coordinate communications, so that one merger partner does not unintentionally contradict the other. Ultimately, any conflict will require both sides to modify their positions, causing irreparable damage. Inconsistency destroys existing brand power, confuses employees and customers, and worries shareholders and potential investors.

Designating a single corporate spokesperson for both sides of a merger signifies that consistency is critical. The "chief communications officer" would report directly to the CEOs and CFOs of the merged partners, representing both concurrently. Clearly, this person must command the universal credibility and confidence of employees, customers, and the financial community.

Communicate the Brand for Keeps

Having initiated your branding program, go on the communications offensive and control the chatter. Your competitors and the marketplace will try to define your new company and its brand. Don't let them. Think carefully about the first year of internal and external postmerger communications. Develop a meticulous, long-term global brand strategy for the newly merged organization, and support it with new corporate communications that accurately represent the new entity. Talk to all your constituencies often and consistently, and plan on doing that for at least three to five years.

When Bell Labs was spun off from AT&T, it was one of the most widely held stocks in the world. Though many might have sat on their laurels, Bell Labs chose to create a new corporate name and to launch an entirely new brand, investing significantly in the effort. Today, Lucent Technologies has a larger market cap than its former parent, AT&T. Supporting the new brand was not only courageous, it was very smart business.

A New Kind of Global Thinking

The world keeps getting smaller, which will profoundly affect mergers and acquisitions. The euro's difficulties will ease and ultimately eliminate many currency issues. Companies will be listed on stock markets worldwide with greater regularity. On-line stock trading will become standard operating procedure. Mergers will include global combinations that few would have believed possible until very recently.

The lesson here: assess and heed the global impact and implications of every single communication.

The Hoechst/Rhône-Poulenc merger, the acquisition of Zenith by LG Electronics, and the Deutsche Bank's takeover of Bankers Trust all reflect the current global merger mentality. These combinations indicate a new kind of global thinking about business: a world without preconceived ideas, a world without barriers and without borders.

Building Bridges

While the cost of getting branding right is not much more than a decimal point on the deal, potential returns can be enormous. So if your company has plans to take advantage of the momentum and visibility a merger or takeover can bring, keep in mind that your brand, like any valuable asset, must be carefully shepherded through the change.

Besides today's staggering number of mergers, acquisitions, and spin-offs, globalization is also helping spawn a new kind of corporate birthing. In a special report in *Business Week*, the point was made that though the world of corporate finance was dominated by takeovers in the 1990s, the next decade and beyond may well be defined by alliances, joint ventures, and partnerships. Throughout the world, companies are building bridges to each other, creating alliances that may not always work but might be the new shape of global business.[3]

These new relationships have their detractors, of course. Some observers claim that partnerships seldom work well and can be difficult to manage. Others cite research studies indicating high rates of failure. Nevertheless, many of us believe that the advent of the alliance and the technology that makes it feasible favorably serve new burgeoning needs and opportunities.

Bottom Line Value

The bottom line question concerning partnerships is: Do they create value? The failure rate is high, but despite this, many senior executives are convinced alliances make strategic sense.

In an article in *Business Week*, Noel Forgeard, CEO of Airbus Industries, a marketing consortium of French, British, and German aerospace companies, stated that European companies are increasingly looking to partnerships to enhance the bottom line. "It is partnerships which have helped create shareholder value," Forgeard said, referring to France's industries in general and Airbus in particular. And: "It is obvious none of the Airbus partners would be able to establish a company on a par with Boeing in a world market by themselves."[4]

The UAL Corporation also has discovered and put to good use the benefits of alliances. Retired chairman and CEO Gerald Greenwald wrote in *Chief Executive Digest*:

Talk of an alliance with even a potential competitor in the airline industry used to be highly unlikely. For the most part, if you were not a friend, you had to be an enemy. . . .

But things changed. . . . Technology got powerful, margins tightened, the world shrunk, and tomorrow demanded a whole new business model. But there is a simpler answer to why alliances have taken off: the customer said so.

Passengers . . . just want to get to their destinations safely, affordably, and with little hassle. . . . An international flight can go wrong at many points—ticketing, baggage, connections, uncomfortable waits in airports, flier miles lost in cyberspace. Alliances provide the opportunity to remove those things from the international traveler's experience. . . . Travelers are going to stay with the airline that can take the pain out of international travel.

No one airline can serve the world . . . but alliances can accomplish a host of achievements that ultimately satisfy the customer and expand the customer base—and provide a higher return on capital:

- Create a globally powerful infrastructure
- Build a fleet of aircraft that is much stronger than the sum of its parts
- Add value with new routes and services
- Share costs
- Streamline operations

We now have marketing partnerships with 19 airlines that enabled United to add 1,447 flights to 110 additional destinations . . . [The Star Alliance]—the first truly global alliance in our industry—is not a substitute for one's own profitability, [nor] a lifeline to keep a struggling airline afloat. An alliance is more like a marriage whose whole must be stronger than the sum of the individual parts.[5]

Customers know what they need and want in seamless global travel. Alliances make it possible for the airlines to give it to them.

Another Internet Marketplace

At this writing, another kind of airline alliance is also being born, one that includes UAL Corp.'s United Airlines. Joining American Airlines, Air France, British Airways, Continental Airlines, and Delta Air Lines in a new on-line marketplace, this mega-alliance will allow carriers and their suppliers to buy and sell all kinds of airline-related goods and ser-

$100 MILLION JOINT VENTURE

One partnership that is bound to catch the attention of the world is an agreement between Toyota Motor Corporation and the Chinese state-run company Tianjin Automobile Xiali Corporation. Yuri Kageyama, writing for the Associated Press, reported that Beijing has approved the Japanese automaker to make up to 30,000 compact cars a year in China in a new joint venture. Toyota hopes this will give it a competitive edge in a growing market.

The $100 million joint venture is tentatively named Tianjin Toyota Motor Co., and ownership will be split evenly between the two partners. The new models designed for the Chinese market will carry the Toyota name and use the same basic structure as the popular Vitz model, sold as the Yaris in Europe. The Toyota Echo, sold in the United States, also uses the same platform.

Seiji Sugiura, auto analyst for Nomura Securities Co. in Tokyo, said that the Chinese market is potentially so massive, there is plenty of room for several automakers to sell cars there: "Given the numbers, Toyota has a reasonable business plan in China. The challenge for the future is coming up with a fresh brand image that truly appeals to Chinese consumers."

Individual drivers are expected to account soon for about half of China's 1.8 million auto market. Toyota vice president Kousuke Yamamoto told reporters: "We expect individual demand in the Chinese market to grow dramatically for high-quality compacts like the ones we are going to be making."

Production at the joint venture will begin in 2002 and employ 500 people. Toyota already operates about 20 projects in China, including an engine plant.

The Chinese government also approved a plan by Toyota to manufacture with Tianjin Xiali in 2001 a redesigned compact model that will be sold under the Tianjin Automotive brand. Tianjin Xiali and Toyota already work together to produce 100,000 Xiali models a year, but production with the redesigned Xiali will grow to 120,000 annually by next year.

vices. By encouraging competition among suppliers, the airlines look to lower their transaction, processing, and inventory costs.

"As an industry, the purchasing process has been unbelievably inefficient," Gregory Brenneman, president and chief operating officer of Continental said. "I think the real savings are going to be from having us all purchasing using a common technology. We're going to save a few forests by this process." The investors, Brenneman added, hope that all the carriers will use the site.

John MacLean, vice president of purchasing for AMR Corp.'s American Airlines, noted that, in addition to cost savings, the site will give carriers greater access to buying opportunities. "We don't know all the sources of products and services in Asia or Europe or the Middle East." Suppliers will be able to plan more accurately because the airlines can now project inventory demand effectively. Patrick Wildenburg, vice president of purchasing for Delta, commented: "Clearly, the ability to integrate buyers and sellers and to have visibility of inventory is key."[6]

The debate over the merits of partnerships and alliances, along with the correlative subject of mergers and takeovers, is too lengthy and complex to cover here. It needs its own book. One thing is clear, however. The company that looks for partners, or looks to be a partner, needs an established brand—a well-conceived, global brand that can help sell its company by communicating clearly and consistently the company's character, purpose, and reputation.

Ten Key Points to Review and Remember

1. Merger activity is still frantic, but mergers can sometimes be dangerous, damaging stock price and engendering confusion, conflict, anger, and uncertainty among employees.

2. The cross-cultural integration process—or rather, the lack of one—is often blamed for merger failure.

3. Four lessons on integration from GE Capital:
   - Begin the integration process before the deal is signed.
   - Dedicate a full-time individual to managing the integration process.

- Implement any necessary restructuring sooner rather than later.
- Integrate not only the business operations, but also the corporate cultures.

4. Making the brand part of the deal is one way to avoid merger breakdown. Because the brand is the spirit of the merger and its value is at the heart of integration, it should be put to work immediately on the company's behalf.

5. Exploit initial interest. Your corporate profile is seldom more visible than during the announcement of a merger or acquisition, so take full advantage of the opportunity to communicate on a grand scale.

6. The importance of your own people cannot be exaggerated. A merger can be unnerving for employees; sometimes they need to be coaxed through the process.

7. Having initiated your branding program, go on the communications offensive and control the chatter. Talk to all your constituencies often and consistently.

8. Assess and heed the global impact and implications of every single communication. Your brand, like any valuable asset, must be carefully shepherded through the various aspects of the merger process.

9. Companies worldwide are building bridges to each other. The defining deal for the next decade and beyond may well be the alliance, the joint venture, the partnership.

10. Alliances can accomplish a host of achievements that ultimately satisfy the customer, expand the customer base, and provide a higher return on capital.

9

The Board and the Brand

As WE HAVE NOTED, there are measures a company can take to overcome various kinds of national barriers to global expansion, whether real or perceived. In a recent study, 80 percent of the American corporations examined and 70 percent of the European currently employ a local national at the head of a majority of their countrywide operations abroad.

In addition, 60 percent of these companies have introduced a foreign perspective through one of the following means: (1) a foreign director, (2) a foreign top executive, or (3) a foreign advisory board.

The board of directors, in particular, is considered by many corporations to offer prime opportunities for fostering a single, favorable cross-border relationship. *Chief Executive Digest* reported that between 1995 and 1998 the number of companies with foreign directors increased from 39 to 60 percent. Companies with three or more nonnational directors increased from 11 to 23 percent. And by 1998, 10 percent of all directors were nonnational, up from 6 percent three years earlier. Given that the number of board members in general has been decreasing, this suggests that nonnational directors are gaining an influential role in boardrooms around the world.[1]

Actually, the number of companies specifying that they want nonnational directors on their boards has increased dramatically in recent years. It is reported that about a third to a half of non-executive directorship searches are now for nonnationals.

The drive for taking on nonnational directors often originates with new management who wish to transform and professionalize the board in order to move the company forward, possibly expanding operations globally or increasing the use of existing assets abroad.

Then, too, many companies, especially in the United States, are reappraising the guidelines that constitute suitable experience for being a board member. In the past, boards normally sought directors with CEO or COO experience, but now at least four factors are shrinking that particular pool of potential candidates:

- Increasingly, sitting CEOs are restricted to that number of outside directorships deemed appropriate.
- The exclusion of insiders in favor of outside directors has caused a reevaluation of interlocking directorates.
- Worldwide merger activity and restructuring has led to more boards being formed from scratch.
- A growing number of corporations are adopting age and term limits for their board members.

The skill sets of board candidates are also being reconsidered. Know-how and specific desired areas of expertise are increasingly the determining factors in selecting board members, rather than the more traditional measure: senior management experience. Understanding that language and cultural nuances are crucial to globalization, required acceptance criteria has been greatly expanded to include pertinent cultural insight.

Theodore Jadick, managing partner, Heidrick & Struggles, compiled the following description of a global outside director:

- Different life experience; raised in different culture with unique educational systems, values, and beliefs
- International career experience; worked in several companies with different responsibilities

- Global outlook; boundaryless view of business issues
- Cultural assimilation; global directors who feel at ease in different cultures, having mastered the nuances of social and business customs
- Career success[2]

I might add to this list of qualifications—although it should be implicit—that the candidate possess a thorough understanding of corporate/global branding, its value and application. He or she should place a high priority on the management of the corporate brand; understand the need for brand custodianship; regard the brand as an important corporate asset; and recognize the link between effective brand management and the effective management of the business.

Obstacles to the Nonnational

There are, however, two major and very practical obstacles to attracting competent nonnational board members. The first of these is the extra time commitment involved in serving on a board, especially if the candidate is still a working manager. For example, will the busy CEO of an Asian company have the time to attend as many as eight or nine board meetings halfway around the world?

Time zones can also present serious problems. The amount of communication required for board meetings—the circulation of agendas and other materials, plus numerous telephone consultations—is usually difficult to coordinate across different time zones.

The other major problem to attracting non-national board members is language. It is generally argued that English has achieved global status. However, there are a great many more speakers of Chinese, Hindi, or Urdu than of English, while the number of Spanish and Arabic speaking peoples are not far behind.

Nevertheless, as companies globalize their boards by recruiting foreign directors, there is an increasing trend to the use of English, now perceived by some as the international business lingua franca. Board meetings for global companies, for example, are often held in English.

Many companies, however, in non-English speaking countries reject this trend and resist changing the language spoken in their boardrooms. This is particularly common in Japan as well as in parts of continental

Europe. But despite these demurrers, an increasing number of companies prefer to have key meetings conducted in English, in the belief that this positions them as being multicultural, international, and even cosmopolitan—a mark of prestige.

Of course, time problems and language differences are not the only obstacles to non-national board members. There are also possible cultural barriers, which can lead to conflicting opinions over appropriate chains of command in terms of information flow, account for divergent ideas on how to run the business, and even create disagreement on the very function of a director.

In spite of the progress of globalization and the advance of the non-national director, many U.S. corporations still leave their multinationalism at the boardroom door—or so it seems, at least, when it comes to appointing Asian directors. Apparently, relatively few Asian executives are willing to cross the Pacific to attend frequent board meetings in the United States. Thus, American companies are more likely to turn to European executives to fill non-national slots on their boards.

Long-Term Plan and Commitment

Global branding is not a hit or miss project. It has to have a long-term plan and commitment, and a real, underlying investment in time and money. Some board members are now insisting that the CEO have an understanding of global branding and a game plan for building it. When they show resolve and when they are wisely led, directors can offer great assistance to a busy CEO. In particular, they can foster a climate that supports, enables, and ultimately demands the full achievement of business potential.

Even so, the CEO must lead the way. He or she has to determine whether the existing company brand can succeed globally, or whether it needs to be modified or replaced. It's up to the chief executive to propose the right plan for the situation at hand and issue clear communications to activate the global branding program and achieve the branding goals. It goes without saying that the CEO also makes sure that each and every board member—national or non-national—understands the branding message communicated.

Whether the CEO is all by himself or herself at the controls of the brand or is aided by a specially designated senior officer, board members are going to look primarily to him or her, not only for a well-defined corporate vision, but also for a well-communicated global brand. The experienced director understands that communication is pivotal to successful branding, and knows it is one of the most powerful weapons in the CEO's arsenal.

Naturally, it is not the board's specific responsibility to create the company brand, but the directors can—and should—act as an attentive and competent sounding board for major corporate messages emanating from the CEO's office. These include all the various forms of brand communication—corporate advertising to product brand advertising, public to investor to employee relations, and everything in between.

Communications must be consistent, and if they're not, the board should demand of the CEO that they should be. Without clear, consistent messages, there can be no effective brand. And because of the varied challenges of local cultures, this is especially true when branding across borders.

Thus, an involved and dedicated board can play an active and helpful role in the global branding process. The directors' various backgrounds and expertise should prove invaluable to the CEO and key to the ultimate effectiveness of the brand and the success of the globalization program.

A Delicate Balance

Disclosure standards in foreign countries are now under pressure to meet the U.S. model. From a Conference Board report:

> To bring disclosure standards up to U.S. levels . . . overseas companies are providing more information to global equity markets. U.S. and non-U.S. systems of governance may meet somewhere in the middle—a move which is expected to achieve that delicate balance between the historic close-to-the-vest relationship of company and institutional investor with the desired candor that inspires confidence. . . .
>
> Increased cross-border transactions are producing new ownership structures, higher expectations, and rapidly changing patterns of communication. . . . Over time, communications between global companies

and their investors will be shaped less by country-specific legal systems. And, as U.S. institutional investors take large positions in non-U.S. corporations, their style of communications will spread.[3]

The Measure of Corporate Governance

Robert Lear, chairman of *Chief Executive*'s Advisory Board, describes corporate governance as "the whole process of running a company and serving the best interests of the shareholders in conformity with the laws and ethics of the land." All the factors involved in balancing the power between the CEO, the board, and the shareholders, he writes, are now considered "part of the corporate governance syndrome."[4]

Corporate governance is finally coming into its own, with a number of companies seeking to improve their governance program and their stockholders' impressions of it. In the past, corporations were criticized for communicating inadequately with shareholders, among other perceived imperfections. Many well-managed companies began answering these criticisms by changing the composition of their boards, giving more power to their outside directors, and disclosing more information to investors.

As a result, an increasing number of corporations now create and publish corporate governance statements. Boards set up special committees to oversee their governance procedures, and, with an eye toward achieving more effective performance, they periodically evaluate both the CEO and themselves.

How does one gauge the adequacy of corporate governance? You may start with good board composition and structure, but these are not the only criteria. The real measure is how well the board members work together, work with management, and work with the shareholders. In effect, it is how well they communicate, despite any individual nationalistic leanings—which also means how well they listen.

If the typical board's focus is on leadership succession, company strategy, and representing constituencies, then it has to understand the attitudes and needs of its owners. A vigorous global board leadership encourages the accomplishment of long-term corporate goals, with specific responsibilities including the origination of mission statements that are clear and to the point, and the creation of policies that support and strengthen the brand.

In what other ways can the board contribute? For one thing, a CEO may involve his or her directors in designing and implementing a strategic measurement process. There indeed seems to be a trend toward more of such board involvements. It may be only a question of governance, but a growing number of boards feel it their responsibility to put into place an effective set of performance measurements and to monitor carefully the resulting evaluations.

Global Business Ethics Codes

Board participation in the institution and monitoring of global business ethics codes is on the increase. Research shows that the formulation of these codes now involves 95 percent of CEOs, 92 percent of general counsels, and 78 percent of boards of directors.

How thoughtfully and capably a company establishes these codes and follows them has relevance to the worldwide success of its corporate brand. And, more often than not, the directors exercise a key influence on the determination of good global business practices.

Ronald E. Berenbeim writes in *Chief Executive Digest*:

> The rapid pace of internationalization of business has been confronting companies with the formidable challenge of formulating and implementing global business practice standards and monitoring them worldwide for effectiveness. . . .
>
> Additionally, the role of outside parties such as nongovernmental organizations (NGOs) and business schools in the development of company ethics programs is now more significant. Many NGOs are now demanding that issues such as environmental responsibility and fair labor practices be addressed. Increasingly, business schools in all parts of the world are including ethics issues and analytic methods in the curricula that are the foundation of management education.
>
> Three trends favor the corporate articulation of global business ethics codes:
>
> - Growing North American and European participation in world markets
> - Necessary role of ethical business climate in improving Asian, African, and Latin American prospects for development
> - Increased emphasis on corporate and individual conduct as well as financial performance

[There is also] a developing consensus worldwide with respect to certain code subject matter. Codes now feature a common subject matter, particularly with regard to contract (e.g., conflict of interest) and legally mandated (e.g., sexual harassment) ethics standards. . . . Many companies now require supplier, vendor, or joint venture partners to comply with certain provisions of their codes.[5]

Monitoring its company's business ethics codes is one critical way in which the board can not only be of significant service, but can also contribute to the advance of the brand and corporate reputation.

A Three-Way Balance of Power

Shareholder relations is still another way today's director can put his or her stamp on the company reputation. Shareholder activism can influence both management and the board to effect desired corporate changes while at the same time increasing board authority and responsiveness. The more information communicated by investors to the board, the greater authority the board can display.

Board members understand more than ever how their companies and corporate brands are perceived by the investment community. As a result, more and more companies make regular presentations to their boards, with the three-way balance of power between management, directors, and shareholders central to communicating strategic corporate performance information.

The board should monitor carefully the corporate persona. Directors are expected to scrutinize management's ability to deliver positive results and, when necessary, act as a change agent. They need to be able to say to the CEO: "We don't believe the company's image is what it should be. We should be able to evaluate our image in some systematic way to learn how we stack up against peer groups." In other words, the board can—and should—generate and communicate ideas of its own.

Communicating Corporate Performance

In examining the best practices for communicating strategic performance-related information, the Conference Board's Second International Working Group studied a number of internal and external channels of corporate communication. Channels included management communication to all employees, management to the board of directors, and shareholders to management and to the board.

Dr. Carolyn Kay Brancato says of these studies that "the process of establishing strategic performance measures must be initiated from the CEO down through the company. Unless this occurs, individual units will not have the authority or 'buy in' to accomplish a company-wide effort.

"Ideally, the process is both top down and bottom up. Companies report the most success instituting strategic performance measurement systems that involve setting strategic goals at the more senior levels, then letting action plans develop at the operating or 'hands-on' levels. . . . The vision must be uniformly communicated throughout the company."[6]

All forms of communication, of course, bear on the company's reputation and corporate brand in one way or another. One important channel of information from the CEO's office to the board is the director of investor relations. In considering how a director of investor relations should deal with the board, there is one significant maxim: make sure your boss, whether he or she is the CEO or the CFO, is kept fully informed of all activities you plan that concern the board.

With this thought in mind, there are a number of communications responsibilities the IR chief should take on with respect to the directors. Among these, naturally, are periodic written and oral reports to the board regarding key investor relations activities. In addition, the investor relations officer will see that board members are invited to financial analyst meetings. He or she will also include the directors on the lists for news release mailings, send them copies of pertinent news items, and alert them in the event important financial news is about to break in the media.

Of equal importance, the functions of all corporate officers are tied in to furthering the company brand in some way. The IR chief has this same responsibility: her or his particular insight and perspective on the brand, the financial events and activities that affect it, and its regard by the investors, will be of special concern to the board.

Get the Board on Board

It's especially critical for the CEO to establish solid relationships with all board members, involving each and every one where possible, and

A NEVER-ENDING GLOBAL SEARCH

In Chapter 5, I pointed out that despite various cultural and language barriers, the real global challenge is the ongoing war between competitors for talented human resources. That search applies to boardroom talent as well. And the search goes on—not only domestically, but around the globe.

With a growing number of companies now recognizing the considerable inroads women have made in domains once purely masculine, competent women senior executives—especially experienced CEOs—are in great demand to fill board vacancies.

James E. Preston, former CEO of Avon Products, pointed out that Avon introduced women to its board in the early 1970s and now has six women serving as directors: "If the company is to understand the market and position products and communications to women, then women must be represented at all levels, starting with the board."[7] Avon obviously takes its own advice: its current CEO is a woman, Andrea Jung.

But why aren't there more women on corporate boards? Julie Daum wrote in *Chief Executive*: "There's no getting away from the fact that boards seek to add directors who can operate on a peer level with others already on the board and have had the experience and seasoning required to be vital contributors to discussions and strategy decisions. Many CEOs feel under pressure to appoint women and are frustrated at their inability to come up with appropriate candidates. . . . Indeed, the relatively few women who meet the spec for directors are besieged by invitations to join boards."[8]

Many such candidates, however, feel that membership on one board is all they can handle properly while continuing to manage their own business. Thus, the relatively small number of women executives whose skills and background do meet typical board requirements accept board invitations with only the greatest care. Then, too, unfortunately, there are still parts of the world where, thanks to gender bias, that invitation may never come.

Even in countries where women executives are readily accepted, many candidates want their boardroom roles to reflect the talent and experience they bring to the table. They don't wish to be viewed as merely token directors. They see board service as a mutually beneficial experience that allows them to develop their own abilities while contributing meaningfully to another company.

strengthening the makeup of the board when necessary. Thus, CEOs are well-advised to work with their boards on all strategic issues, but most certainly in the area of strategic performance measures. In this way they can better align the company's interests in dealing with outside shareholders.

In building relationships with his or her directors, the chief executive officer has certain procedures to consider—procedures that are always useful, but are particularly indispensable for a new CEO. For one thing, the CEO should meet personally with each board member as soon as possible after appointment to discuss concerns, hopes, and ideas for the company and the brand's future success. Directors are usually delighted to have their opinions actively solicited in this manner, and it helps establish the beginning of constructive, positive relationships.

The strength of the board is hypercritical to the success of a new CEO and his or her vision for the company. The new CEO should be able to expect full support and aid from each director. This means communication lines must be kept open and well lubricated. If the CEO finds that a board member does not provide the help and suggestions looked for, or does not understand or approve the corporate mission strategy, the CEO should make whatever changes necessary, from working to improve the director's performance to replacing the board member altogether.

Today's corporate leader encounters a variety of different audiences whose acceptance must be earned on a continuing basis. The gaining of this acceptance is, of course, the prime mission of the corporate/global brand. And because most CEOs cite the board as their most significant constituency, it's crucial that each individual board member know and fully understand the branding message. This is obviously a key assignment, one best handled by the CEO, as steward of the brand.

Ten Key Points to Review and Remember

1. The board of directors is considered by many corporations to offer prime opportunities for fostering a single, favorable cross-borders relationship.

2. The number of companies specifying non-national directors on their boards has increased dramatically. Trends driving this search include:
   - Professionalizing of boards
   - Widening the overall pool of potential candidates
   - Reconsidering the necessary skills for becoming a director

3. In the past, companies normally sought directors with CEO or COO experience, but that particular pool of potential candidates is shrinking.

4. Two major obstacles stand in the way of attracting competent non-nationals to the board: the extra time commitment involved and potential language problems.

5. Global branding has to have a long-term plan and commitment and a real, underlying investment in time and money. Wisely led, directors can offer great assistance to a busy CEO by fostering a climate that supports, enables, and demands the full achievement of business potential.

6. All of the factors involved in balancing the power between the CEO, the board, and the shareholders are now considered part of the corporate governance syndrome.

7. Board participation in the institution and in monitoring global business ethics codes is on the increase. Formulation entails conducting an organizational analysis, drafting a code of global business conduct, and creating an awareness of the code through training.

8. There is a developing consensus regarding the key organizing principles of these codes:
- Fixed reference points required
- Utilization of ethical decision-making procedures
- An employment environment of mutual trust

9. In the ongoing war for talented human resources, the search also applies to boardroom talent, and qualified women executives should be included in this search.

10. It is critical for the CEO to establish solid relationships with all board members, involving each wherever possible and strengthening board makeup when necessary.

10

Brands in Decline, Protests, and Assorted Crises

SURPRISING AS IT may seem, some of the best known brands in corporate America are losing their luster, actually declining in potency—perhaps a signal that even the strongest Old Economy reputation is no guarantee against the perceived allure of the New Economy.

I find this extraordinary, and I don't believe this shift is a onetime phenomenon. Clearly, the rules of branding are changing, and now is not the time to become comfortable with a brand's historic position. With unemployment down to only 4 percent and inflation at an all-time low as I write, there is a willingness on the part of investors to take huge risks in innovative information technology. This, along with cost cutting by business and government, increases flexibility and efficiency, resulting in the faster growth and lower inflation of the New Economy.

Despite a boom at the time, a recent Corporate Branding study indicated that companies with such global powerhouse brands as Coca-Cola, Walt Disney, General Electric, FedEx, and Procter & Gamble suffered unprecedented drops in potency in 1999, compared with 1998. We've never seen such traditionally powerful brands so weakened in a single year before.

While big brands suffered in this particular survey, weaker brands on average gained considerable clout. Companies with relatively obscure brand names such as Paccar, Transatlantic Holdings, MagneTek, and C. R. Bard made sharp gains.

A disenchantment with blue-chip stocks and a desire for better growth opportunities were driving factors behind the decline of the more familiar brands and the rise of newer ones. Investors were emboldened to seek new opportunities. Plus, the incredible push for consumer and investor attention by many New Economy brands—such as America Online, Yahoo, Netscape, and eBay—overwhelmed older brands.

To add to their woes, attempts by older brands to recast themselves as young and "hip" fell flat. Putting a "dot.com" after a familiar brand—just to look younger—is usually bad news and in today's volatile market can be suicidal.

The decline in investor attraction is only one reason, of course, that many of the traditional blue-chip brands lose out in the competition for the investment dollar.

Coca-Cola, for example, has had some special, localized problems of their own. Due to a contamination scare in the summer of 1999, Coke withdrew products from three European countries: Belgium, France, and Poland. These were actually separate, isolated incidents, but they compounded the problem with their inauspicious timing.

In reporting the story, *Ad Age International* said: "Well-known for experimenting with many different creative agencies, Coke's response to the contamination crisis, widely regarded as too little too late, has lacked a coordinated agency response." As a result, it also seems to have lacked a coordinated media approach.

When several hundred children in Belgium became ill after drinking Coke products, the company took out a newspaper ad in which Coke's chairman said, "I should have spoken to you earlier." After this belated response to the problem, Coke and ad agency Publicis delivered vouchers and coupons for one free family-size bottle of Coke to each of Belgium's 4.4 million homes, and publicized its offer in another newspaper ad.

In France, when the government lifted its ban on Coke products, the company quickly aired a U.S. commercial, adapted for France, with the catchline: "Today, more than ever, we thank you for your loyalty."

In Poland, a precipitous newspaper ad guaranteed the integrity of locally produced Coke products. Unfortunately, dead mold was found inside bottles of Bonaqua, Coke's local mineral water, and there was a drop of up to 7 percent in the number of unit cases sold afterward.[1]

The contamination scare certainly may have contributed to the decline of Coca-Cola's brand power. Was it solely responsible? No, but it didn't help. Nor did the uncoordinated, multiagency advertising approach that followed. Of course, that's not the whole story. In this highly complex New Economy, many factors can help erode a brand. It's said that Coke is scaling down its global ambitions and embarking on the biggest restructuring in its history in response to two years of sagging earnings.

As I write this, *Business Week* reports that major changes have been made in Coke's Euro marketing equation. Coca-Cola's new CEO, Douglas N. Daft, is working hard and fast to adopt a more localized marketing plan, with particular emphasis on Europe. The changes will encompass advertising, packaging, and even products, which will no longer be dictated out of the home office. "We used to make TV commercials in Atlanta for China," Daft said. "That's not appropriate."

Coke has selected Europe for its new experiments in localism—an approach Daft had successfully tried in Japan. The strategy so far has improved Coke's image in Europe, but European sales are not yet meeting expectations.

"The crisis had taught us the need to get closer to local consumers," said Marc Mathieu, president of Coca-Cola's new Benelux and France division. Having been structured as a single division before, Daft broke Europe into 10 geographic groups. No longer dominated by headquarters, non-Americans now run 9 of Coke's 10 new European groups. "The new teams," Mathieu said, "are developing flavors with distinctly European appeal."[2]

For example, the Turkish division has introduced a new pear-flavored drink, while the German operation has come out with a berry-flavored Fanta. And Coke's local managers now enjoy new freedom in marketing these products.

Before this new localism, Atlanta would even prevent individual divisions from setting up their own websites. They were allowed to use only the corporate Internet home page—not a very satisfactory arrangement.

Now, marketing directors for European divisions can set up their own sites. Among others, there is now a Belgian website. Available in Dutch, French, and English, it draws more than 3 million hits a month.

Coke's new program of local marketing in Europe has yet to produce the gains in sales hoped for. But polls do show that European consumers are less angry over last year's contamination scare. By giving its Euro managers a new marketing freedom, Coke is definitely looking for sales to climb—and soon.

An Unrealistic Premise?

Some analysts believe that global branding is on the wane, pointing out the decline of many big brands. They feel that global branding is based on the unrealistic premise that the whole world can unite in wanting one particular brand. It's not so easy, however, to eliminate successful local brands.

James Brandman and Kathryn Hanes, writing in *Global Finance*, said: "These global brand owners have learned the hard way that the potential of new markets—particularly emerging markets—is not easy to harness. They felt the brunt of the Asian financial crisis in the third quarter of 1998 when consumer goods volumes fell to insufficient levels to justify the heavy cost of building distribution systems and marketing. For global brand owners in emerging markets, there are also issues of affordability, national identity, and preference for domestic products."[3]

It's really not surprising that some corporations with global brands are beginning to believe that one possible answer to overseas expansion might simply be to buy up the local brands. For them this may seem the easiest way to crack new markets, but developing nations usually resent such moves.

Brand Battered by a Backlash

There are various reasons why a company might lose brand power. A contamination scare like Coke's is only one. For another, sometimes a company will suddenly strike out in a totally new direction, ignoring its traditional vision and overlooking its hard-won corporate brand.

Consider Monsanto. A well-regarded commodity chemicals company for close to a century, it suddenly veered off into life-science businesses. CEO Robert Shapiro, quoted in the *Wall Street Journal*, envisioned his company "as a biotechnology factory on the cutting edge, churning out novel foods and medicines." The traditional commodity chemicals business was spun off, leaving the company free to explore the potentials of biotechnology.

The *Journal* commented: "Billions of dollars later, that concept of a unified 'life sciences' company—using technology to improve both medicines and foods—has become an affliction itself for Monsanto. The crop-biotechnology half of the program has grown so controversial that Monsanto has agreed to a deal that is likely not only to push biotech to the back burner, but also cost Monsanto its independence. And investors are reacting harshly. Monsanto's agreement to combine with Pharmacia & Upjohn Inc. is billed as a merger of equals, but it leaves the Pharmacia side with the upper hand."[4]

During his program's planning stages, Shapiro conferred with environmentalists, envisioning the ecological good his venture could produce. Yet it was the environmentalists, fearful of possible unintentional consequences, who organized stormy opposition to Shapiro's plans for genetically modified food.

For all of his attention to the subject of genetically engineered plants, Shapiro neglected one critical issue: Monsanto knew very little about the potential customers for genetically modified food—grocery shoppers. Crop biotechnology can create plants that are easier and cheaper for farmers to grow, but middle-class consumers normally won't be impressed—especially if they are not convinced that the food is safe to eat.

During the years Monsanto manufactured commodity chemicals like carpet fiber, its marketing programs generally stayed in the background. It seems evident that Shapiro had no clear marketing and/or communications plan to gain public acceptance of bioengineered food.

In the summer of 1999, European environmental groups fervently opposed to genetically modified foods began to heighten awareness of the issue in the U.S. They argued that such crops risked releasing genes inadvertently into the environment with unpredictable effects. Regulators, including the Food and Drug Administration, had not yet focused on genetically modified crops, having no particular reason to believe they were unsafe to eat. Safe or not, surveys now show that the vast majority of Americans want genetically altered foods identified as such on their labels.

The *Wall Street Journal* concluded: "And how does Mr. Shapiro feel, seeing a vision he figured could serve both humanity and shareholders come under such attack—its products labeled 'Frankenfoods' and the company demonized as 'Monsatan'? He leaves no doubt of how misguided he thinks the environmental activists opposing genetically modified food are."[5]

Open Markets

Investment in risky innovation, a driver of the New Economy, depends on open global markets. These days, national markets simply do not provide rewards large enough for entrepreneurs who take uncertain chances. That domestic markets must be open to foreign trade is therefore necessary. Without vigorous overseas competition, many companies will make changes slowly, almost grudgingly.

It should be noted, especially after the demonstrations against the World Trade Organization in Seattle, that advocacy groups—not only in the U.S. but abroad—feel threatened by free trade. In fact, Europe has had even more demonstrations than the United States against corporate-driven globalization.

Citizens facing globalization worry that powerful corporations will override national sovereignty and undermine political and monetary systems. Activists are also seriously troubled by the sweatshop labor practices in many lands, the outsourcing of factory jobs, and corporate investment in countries with brutal, despotic governments.

In the 1990s some groups began to pressure corporations to make amends for perceived acts of social injustice. Have they had any success? Ask Monsanto. Or Nike. But environmental issues and appalling labor conditions are not the only reasons for activist interest. Nor is that interest necessarily always justified. Take McDonald's.

A McDonald's near Antwerp, Belgium, was destroyed in one of several attacks. In France a number of McDonald's have been vandalized. The French have even made a hero of one farmer who struck out at McDonald's, not so much because they hate the company, but because many believe that multinationals crush local culture.

"We are attacked because we are a number one global, American brand," said a McDonald's spokeswoman in Europe, Alessandra di Montezemolo. "But people should understand we are local partners in the national economies."

McDonald's operates 750 restaurants in France. It attempted to answer protests there by issuing a statement that "80 percent of the products we serve are made in France [and] they are cooked by local employees."

As Roger Cohen of the *New York Times* put it: " . . . *la France profonde* . . . was not impressed.

"Said Patrice Vidieu, the secretary general of . . . a growing farmers' movement: 'What we reject is the idea that the power of the marketplace becomes the dominant force in all societies, and that multinationals like McDonald's or Monsanto come to impose the food we eat and the seeds we plant.' "[6]

Buoyed by early successes, activists undoubtedly will continue to make global corporations the focus of their causes, targeting them for public scrutiny. At times like this, a clear, consistent brand is indispensable as a first line of corporate defense.

Monsanto missed the point. It moved, perhaps too quickly, from commodity chemicals to genetically modified foods without carefully exploring the many ramifications of such a step—without ensuring that its brand was still appropriate and steadfast around the world.

Nike Just Ain't Cool

Nike, one of the most visible brands in the world, has found special obstacles in the path of worldwide brand maintenance and development. When an outcry over labor practices in Nike's overseas factories erupted in the late 1990s, company chairman and cofounder Philip Knight initially glossed over the complaints. But as protests escalated—especially on college campuses and among certain advocacy groups—Knight was compelled to establish new priorities.

Early on, Knight brought in Maria Eitel from Microsoft as vice president for corporate responsibility, and he beefed up management ranks with other talented outsiders who had experience at PepsiCo, Microsoft, and Disney.

Louise Lee wrote in *Business Week*: "The backlash against Nike's labor practices isn't the only crisis the company faces. Two years ago, jolted by shifting teen fashions and the Asian economic downturn, sales of its sneakers and sports apparel hit a brick wall, and the hard times aren't over. . . . Important retail chains are closing stores and the strong dollar is resulting in unfavorable currency translations."

Business Week offered a fitting commentary: "Says Marian Salzman, who heads the Brand Futures Group at Young & Rubicam Inc.: 'Nike just ain't cool.' "[7] What went wrong? Accusations of sweatshop factory conditions overseas certainly didn't help. But there were also basic marketing problems. Uninspired advertising, various fashion blunders, and even too great a use of the swoosh all contributed to Nike's damaged image. In an effort to right things, Nike now pays greater attention to what kids say they're interested in, instead of assuming it already knows.

The biggest single blow to brand Nike has been the bitter controversy surrounding the working conditions in its overseas factories. Company management was taken by surprise by the hostility of the anti-Nike sentiment about its overseas workers. The damage to the brand was real, and in more areas than merely college campuses.

Chairman Knight changed tactics, choosing to engage critics rather than just saying they're wrong. Maintaining that it has made real progress on the issue, Nike cites a literacy program it has started for workers in Indonesia, and claims that even activists acknowledge some improvements in working conditions.

Don't Doubt Activists' Clout

Corporate CEOs might do well to heed the message that comes from the well-publicized World Trade Organization meeting in Seattle in 1999, as well as the September 2000 meetings of the World Bank and IMF in Prague, and the earlier World Economic Forum in Davos, Switzerland. Such pertinacity—exhibited not only by union workers and college students, but by a number of public advocacy groups—may well escalate.

Activists can only be emboldened by the attention they have received. They are opposed to what they view as multinational corporate exploitation of Asian and Latin American workers and the overseas environment, and they look to broaden North American and European standards to include Third World societies.

Jeffrey E. Garten wrote in the *Wall Street Journal*:

> They will target more companies for public scrutiny about their activities abroad, from their environmental policies to their employment practices to their investments in local communities. If you doubt their clout, recall how they pressured Nike to change its sourcing practices, Monsanto its genetically modified products. . . .
>
> There are several reasons why these groups will turn up the heat on multinational companies. The slow moving World Trade Organization will not provide as juicy a target without the world's trade ministers gathering in one place, something that happens only every two years. Global companies are easier targets. They are highly visible; they have made big fixed investments and can't run away. . . .
>
> They are vulnerable because much of their success depends on the integrity of their brands and reputations. And many advocacy groups have learned to maximize their clout by using the Internet to build coalitions around the world.[8]

An Issue of Survival

Success depends on the integrity of the brand, and to protect their global brands and gain the full cooperation of the local communities where they operate, CEOs of global companies need to go well beyond basic public relations strategies. They must find more ways to improve the business and social environments around them. Being a good corporate citizen, with an appropriate corporate image, means establishing specific goals, such as less pollution, more educational opportunities for employees, and so forth.

Such policy objectives ought to be developed inclusively—working not only with employees, but with local customers and suppliers, advocacy groups, governmental agencies, media, and others in the local community. And they should be carried out assiduously. One company that has done this with particular success is BP/Amoco.

Again from the *Wall Street Journal*:

> Sir John Browne, BP/Amoco's CEO, has charged his executives throughout emerging markets to develop community building programs, from training local workers to building local transport systems. The executives' success in such efforts is one factor in determining their pay. . . .

At a time when public opinion about globalization is ambivalent and unpredictable, and when communication is instant and global, a company's relationships with an ever wider group of constituencies are becoming more delicate and more crucial to its long-term market value. For global CEOs, this isn't an issue of ideology but one of survival.[9]

Incubator for Crisis

"Survival" may well be the operative word. The global economy is certainly not entirely healthy. Sixty thousand protesters at Seattle's 1999 WTO meeting should not be written off simply as wild-eyed radicals, jamming streets and smashing windows. Think of them rather as a critical milepost, denoting a basic change in public attitudes. Especially, don't misjudge their movement as either local or one-shot.

That World Trade Organization meeting was simply the occasion where these particular activists burst onto the American conscience. A number of social movements around the world had already connected into grass roots networks, made possible by the astonishing speed of Internet communication.

The fact is, globalization, as we know it, does not reward everyone—nor every company. For one thing, global poverty has intensified, with more than a billion people now living squalid lives, while the rich get richer. Worsening global economic and social inequities could well become a distressing incubator for continual worldwide crisis.

There are those who believe that the promise of globalization only means a race to the bottom for many of the world's peoples. It's their viewpoint that global companies pit workers, communities, and even entire countries against each other to see who will provide the lowest wages and cheapest costs. Their impression is that even when some community or country seems to be getting ahead, it is in reality being driven down to the level of the poorest and most desperate. Thus, activists insist that the reform of the global economy must include human rights for all, a sustained environment worldwide, economic advancement for the oppressed, and democracy at every level.

Global Conspiracy?

There is then a coalition of free-trade skeptics who look to slow the march of globalization. This loose-knit alliance includes environmentalists, unions, farmers, civil and human rights workers, and a broad base of consumer groups as well. They seem to want a global economy where gains in wealth go directly to "the people," advocating, for example, a complete curtailing of globalization and the abolishment of the IMF and World Bank.

Business Week quoted activist Lori Wallach, founder of the Citizens Trade Campaign, saying: "We are not a campaign. We are a mainstream public-interest movement, and we are not going to go away."

However, Paul Magnusson counters: "Wallach insists that the coalition's lobbying strength comes from its message. But critics of the message find it muddled and sometimes contradictory. At the WTO protests in Seattle, some demonstrators demanded stronger enforcement of environmental and labor standards by the WTO, while others sought to dismantle [the organization]. Some opposed the WTO's bias toward securing intellectual-property protections for wealthy nations at the expense of the developing world. But few demonstrators seemed worried about protectionist barriers to imports of textiles and commodities from poorer nations."[10]

Victims of Their Own Largesse

Historically, large corporations have always been accused—especially by the disadvantaged—of being the underlying cause behind all their troubles, economic ones in particular. Today's global corporation is an even bigger target than before. One explanation is the remarkable speed at which multinationals have been expanding abroad, buying out some local businesses while forcing others to the wall.

This is an aspect of globalization that is highly visible, and threatening as well. It goes without saying that such obvious power and influence should be used always with care. Yet even the best intentioned and most carefully laid corporate plans to assist developing nations may irritate activists. Nor are business plans necessarily entirely altruistic.

The strength of the grass roots movement challenging the development and communication of multinational brands is examined by journalist Naomi Klein in her book *No Logo: Taking Aim at the Brand Bullies*. James Ledbetter, in the *New York Times Book Review*, summarized her thesis as one in which "global corporations are often victims of their own image building largess. In their brazen attempts to capture the youth market, companies like Benetton, Calvin Klein, and Nike have very loudly identified their brands with do-gooder goals like equality and tolerance.

"Such bold brand expressions set the bar for corporate behavior quite high. Marketing now adopts 'complex, essential social ideas, for which many people have spent lifetimes fighting,' author Klein explains. 'That's what lends righteousness to the rage of activists campaigning against what they see as cynical distortions of those ideas.' "[11]

In all fairness, Klein seems to hold marketers, brand owners, and even brand consultants in contempt. Another review of Klein's book, written for *The Journal of Brand Management*, says her thesis "claims that a radical new political culture is emerging through schools and colleges, all aimed at keeping brands and corporations out. Well, when wasn't there student rebellion about something?. . . .

"There's no doubt that poor labor conditions should not be tolerated and that corporations have moral and ethical responsibilities, even if the shareholders don't see it that way. But there's no acknowledgment from Klein that maybe, just maybe, some of the workers have benefited from jobs, education programs and so on. . . . It's in the minds of consumers that brands exist in the first place, so perhaps Klein is looking in the wrong place for utopia."[12]

Listen and Do No Harm

The balance of global business power is elusive. Corporations seem to come and go at great pace: one-third of the giants in America's Fortune 500 in 1980 had lost their independence by 1990, and another 40 percent were gone five years later. Globalization is as much a threat to large companies as it is to small, and is often a blessing for those hot little firms that create so much of today's employment and wealth.

The mergers that cause so many excited headlines often only demonstrate defensive moves by the corporate establishment rather than the grasping efforts of global gangsters.

Global corporations should continue to listen to their constituencies, and at the same time try to do no harm. They should take advantage of the responsibilities that go with size and wealth and power. Companies can do much good by spreading wealth, work, and the new technologies that improve production, distribution, and living standards around the world.

Despite postulated doom and gloom—and the zealous opposition both of domestic pressure groups and those developing nations that believe their own economies and companies are being threatened—most of the world's biggest corporations undoubtedly will continue advancing their brands across borders and further expand their global presence. They should.

The global New Economy is going to take time to emerge fully. There may still be misgivings in some places, of course, about the U.S. model of free-market capitalism. Counterbalancing this, however, is the desire for faster growth and a fear of being left behind as the rest of the world starts to embrace the benefits of technology-driven expansion.

By itself, the worldwide proliferation of mobile phones and the Internet cannot create a more vibrant global economy. Also needed are dramatic changes in core institutions that will translate technology into a faster growth of productivity.

Using advanced technology and inspired management techniques, and sustained by a global vision, the world's largest companies are now forging alliances and developing businesses that transcend national borders. It is to be hoped that such activity will spread rather than concentrate the prosperity generated.

Ten Key Points to Review and Remember

1. Some of the best known, strongest brands in America are losing their luster, actually declining in power, although weaker brands, on average, are gaining.

2. Investor disenchantment with blue-chip stocks and a desire for better growth opportunities are considered driving factors behind these changes.

3. Coca-Cola, after three recent, isolated contamination scares, has localized its approach to European marketing, giving local managers more autonomy, and thus more power to handle specific situations, in advertising, promotion, and even products.

4. Some corporations with global aspirations now believe that one answer to overseas expansion might simply be to buy up local brands.

5. One way for a company to lose brand power is to strike out in a new direction, ignoring its traditional vision and overlooking its hard-won corporate brand.

6. Advocacy groups in many countries now feel threatened by globalization and free trade, as well as by certain company labor and environmental practices, and they are actively demonstrating against them.

7. Global companies are easy targets because they are highly visible, can't run away, and so much depends on the integrity of their brands and reputations.

8. CEOs of global companies must search for more ways to improve the business and social environments around them—setting sincere, concrete goals to pollute less, provide educational opportunities for employees, and so forth.

9. However, global corporations are often victims of their own image-building largess, identifying their brands with such "do-gooder" objectives as equality and tolerance. Angry activists campaign against what they see as cynical distortions of those ideas.

10. Multinationals should continue to listen, to try to do no harm, to accept the responsibilities that go with size and wealth—and should continue advancing their brands across borders.

11

Digital Asset Management: Tool for Global Branding

As I HAVE ALREADY pointed out, the advance of technology—with particular emphasis on the Internet—is not only changing how companies compete in the global marketplace, but is compelling customers to rely more on brands to guide their buying choices.

In fact, the Internet economy is changing just about everything we do—at home and abroad. But this provocative global medium is more than just a new technology. It's a revolution in itself—a radical change in the way companies conduct business, with a phenomenal impact on the way we are able to promote and manage brands around the world.

Digital Asset Management (DAM) helps an organization take greater advantage of Internet expediency. It not only provides the opportunity to improve and streamline business processes—reducing costs and increasing efficiencies—but also strengthens the corporate brand through corporate websites, strategic on-line partnerships, on-line promotion, and unique E-commerce solutions.

An On-line Library

Digital Asset Management is simply a tool for organizing digital media assets for storage and retrieval. It is actually an on-line library system, facilitating the management and distribution of digital assets across an organization. It allows the organization to reuse artwork and text—in their latest, most up-to-date versions—in a variety of media, including the Web, video, and print, and without the usual expense in both dollars and time of recreating these valuable assets.

It should be noted here that despite the rapid growth of the Internet for information exchange and advertising, the need for printed materials is actually increasing, thanks in large part to ongoing economic prosperity, increasing population, and greater advertising expenditures.

A company can use DAM to manage corporate communications centrally, providing secure access to intellectual property via a Web browser, and thus ensuring message consistency and brand integrity. The process ensures that only approved brand elements are used, and that they're used in proper context. No wonder DAM is considered by many to be an important management tool—the next major phase in the implementation and control of brand expression.

Savings in Time and Money

Teri Ross, author and consultant, writes in techexchange.com:

> As the [sewn products] industry evolves into technology-driven businesses, an increasing number of companies are reaching a critical pain threshold in needing to control and manage their vast amounts of digital media assets. Technically speaking, a digital asset is any form of media that has been turned into a binary source.
>
> Digital assets, which for textile mills include everything from artwork, logos, and photos to PowerPoint presentations, text documents, and even E-mail, are proving to be valuable assets in terms of both productivity and company valuation. However, an asset is only an asset when you can find it, or you know that you have it in the first place. . . .
>
> Digital Asset Management (DAM) saves not just time but money. Research indicates that the ROI on DAM is between 8:1 to 14:1. Where do the savings come from? Labor reduction is a primary contribution,

allowing employees to spend less time locating assets and more time working on current projects.

Repurposing is another key benefit. The ability to find and research existing work facilitates the reuse of valuable creative assets from previous projects. A by-product of this benefit is faster development. The ability to take advantage of work performed on prior projects will reduce turnaround time. And last, but not least, workflow efficiency—DAM enforces a consistent workflow.[1]

Impact on Brand Management

Establishing and protecting brand identity is especially crucial in today's highly competitive global marketplace. Logos, images, and all forms of marketing collateral must be safeguarded from unauthorized use. At the same time, a company needs to be certain that creative, sales, marketing, and business communications teams can access these digital assets easily whenever needed.

A Digital Asset Management system stores, retrieves, shares, and distributes logos, documents, design templates, etc.—reliably, securely, globally—thereby allowing greater, centralized control of valuable brand assets. Such a system can also speed time to market, eliminate redundancies, improve competitive advantage, and guarantee the accuracy of the materials used. In brief, a DAM system permits the proper reuse and repurposing of visual and textual elements for a variety of media all over the world.

It's often said that a well-managed brand can be a corporation's most powerful business asset, capable of influencing financial performance, even stock price, advantageously. Corporate Branding has found that the company that fully understands brand dynamics, communicates its brand message clearly and consistently, and successfully manages its communications process over time and distance, is able to impact its bottom line measurably and profitably.

A Digital Asset Management system provides the necessary control over corporate identity and other communications assets. It can be central to managing your corporate brand and the overall impression your company makes on customers, employees, investors, the media, and other audiences at home and abroad.

Two Keys: Consistency and Relevance

Consistent representation of the brand is always essential—consistent messages, consistent advertising, consistent experiences for target constituencies. Digital Asset Management is invaluable for ensuring this consistency in all forms of brand communications. It assures adherence to corporate identity guidelines and can be the platform from which all corporate brand communications spring.

Visual elements and brand messages contained within the DAM system have been approved for use, and so promote the standardization of logo applications as well as continuity of design and the use of color, typography, and imagery. By safeguarding this consistency in brand messaging, DAM reinforces the brand image and creates the appearance of seamlessness across company departments, divisions, subsidiaries, and geographic borders.

Not only does it assure consistency, but DAM helps create targeted and relevant branding campaigns. With an increasingly crowded and competitive global marketplace, a brand needs to be more meaningful and convincing for its customers than ever before in order to survive. A brand should address some specific need or want—must make sense to the customer on an individual level.

With DAM it makes no difference if customers and other company targets are located in different regions, different countries, or even different continents. The corporate branding message is going to look the same, feel the same, be the same.

DAM: A Concept for the Future

There are corporations large enough and experienced enough to create their own Digital Asset Management systems. But there are also a number of outside firms that offer the service. One such provider is Cirqit.com, a leading application service provider (ASP) that enhances the way in which companies streamline the life cycle of global business communications.

Many Fortune 2000 companies use Cirqit.com's suite of systems to procure, produce, deliver, and manage all aspects of printed and digital communications, including ordering, storing, fulfilling, customizing, personalizing, and delivering globally.

Cirqit.com offers as the core component of an integrated suite of Web applications a Digital Asset Management system called D.A.M.-It. The system allows a client company to store, categorize, and retrieve corporate images and text—globally, reliably, securely. Cirqit.com is given full command of all its client's digital assets and they are in charge of access management, version control, administration, archiving, and distribution.

Access to real-time customer relationship management (CRM) solutions ensure that an organization can customize and personalize its business communications to meet specific customer needs, buying behaviors, and communications preferences. As a result, companies can produce business communications that drive customer relationships, maximize brand equity, and speed time to market.

D.A.M.-It automates asset management for multiple file formats, incorporates a powerful search engine, and provides comprehensive reporting capabilities to help locate, manage, and track assets across an entire organization. In other words, with a Digital Asset Management system like D.A.M.-It, a company can ensure that the right people get the right asset material at the right time—every time.

A Scalable Suite of Applications

Digital Asset Management will undoubtedly open the branding and communications doors even wider for the global corporation and show the way to successful corporate websites. This seems markedly evident by the recent joining of Cirqit.com with Ariba Supplier Link. The Ariba supplier partner initiative is designed to make goods and services more readily available to corporate buyers and B2B marketplaces on the Internet.

"In today's Internet economy, Fortune 2000 organizations can't afford to have documentation delays hinder their go-to-market strategies," says Jeff Kaufman, former president, CEO, and founding partner of Cirqit.com. "Now companies see that merely finding and reaching their customers is not enough. To succeed, companies must develop, build, and maintain one-to-one, on-line, and traditional customer relationships through the management of a global brand."[2] By offering a scalable suite of applications to automate the print and fulfillment process as well as to connect to an advanced set of DAM customization, personalization, and eCollaboration applications, Cirqit.com has answered those needs. Through the Ariba Supplier Link, Cirqit.com's systems enable corporate buyers to speed and manage the print and digital communication process from start to finish.

As experienced and capable as any single vendor of Digital Asset Management may prove, however, bear in mind that no single provider may necessarily solve all your needs. If you go outside your own organization for Digital Asset Management, you may wish to integrate components from more than one provider into your system because as your needs for DAM grow, they may also change, calling upon new techniques and solutions.

The advancing use of Digital Asset Management is, of course, only one factor to be considered in the future of global branding. Tomorrow's branding world will reflect many other changes and opportunities. The next and final chapter addresses some of the more pertinent.

Ten Key Points to Review and Remember

1. The Internet is making radical changes in the way companies conduct business—with a particular impact on the way they promote and manage brands around the world.

2. In today's Internet economy, large organizations can't afford to have documentation delays and inaccuracies hinder their go-to-market strategies.

3. Digital Asset Management (DAM) is an on-line library system facilitating the management and distribution of digital media assets across an organization.

4. DAM provides secure access to intellectual property, thus ensuring message consistency and brand integrity.

5. Digital assets can include everything from artwork, logos, photos, and text documents to video and even E-mail and PowerPoint presentations.

6. DAM saves both time and money, allowing employees to spend less time locating assets and more time working on current projects.

7. Repurposing is another advantage of Digital Asset Management, as it facilitates the reuse of valuable creative assets from previous projects.

8. A DAM system speeds time to market, eliminates redundancies, improves competitive advantage, and guarantees the accuracy and timeliness of materials used for a variety of media all over the world.

9. Digital Asset Management is invaluable for ensuring consistency and relevance in all forms of brand communications, thus giving the appearance of seamlessness across company departments, divisions, subsidiaries, and geographic borders.

10. Many corporations are large enough to create their own DAM systems, but there are also a number of vendor firms that offer the service.

12

Focus on the Future

PREDICTING THE FUTURE is dicey, but we can always count on change, whatever else this new millennium may bring. More than ever, change is the constant, shattering conventional wisdom, raising standards, toppling traditions. The last decade of the twentieth century witnessed unprecedented political, social, and technological upheaval.

What will drive the economy of the twenty-first century? It's fair to say that the competitive environment is going to be a good deal different from what we've been used to. A great many factors will bear on its evolution, but I would like to touch on three especially influential drivers: the burgeoning information revolution, the birth of exciting new industries, and the expansion of the global marketplace.

It seems sure that the information revolution will continue apace, further boosting productivity. The industries that are the most information-intensive, such as media, finance, and wholesale and retail trade, will experience the greatest changes. In the words of Gerald Greenwald, retired chairman and CEO of UAL Corporation: "Information technology has knocked down the old barriers of time and distance and organizational boundaries."[1]

The information sector continues to be an increasingly powerful factor in advancing growth. The growing number of patents issued strongly indicates that technological innovation has not slowed, which bodes well for years to come. This rapid escalation of technology has the power to eradicate not only national borders, but human ones as well.

A steady stream of technology breakthroughs are creating—and should continue to create—new products, new markets, new companies. Important new industries will spring up, too. Some will undoubtedly be in the field of biotechnology and will have a radical effect on agriculture and health care. Another potential area of industrial growth, microelectromechanical systems (MEMS), should be a major force in food processing, transportation, and home appliances.

And, of course, globalization will be an important driver of the twenty-first century economy. It will provide both larger markets and tougher foreign competitors in the new century. Despite possible soft spots—the recent severe slump in Asia, for instance—long-term trends, at this writing, seem to indicate upward moving trade and rising world incomes.

The company that looks to master tomorrow's worldwide markets and survive rugged competition will find new ways to keep costs down while relying more than ever on innovation to solve many of the problems of the twenty-first century. This includes making every effort to plan, execute, and maintain a powerful, clear-cut, international branding strategy, and communicate it convincingly and faithfully to all constituencies.

Jonathon Gould, senior vice president at MasterCard, foresees an increase in global brands rather than regional brands, and that new names, such as Nokia and Ericsson, will become household brands in just a few years. However, he also feels that the creation of the brand must be separated from its maintenance. A disaster—like the extensive tire recall at Firestone, for instance—quickly causes a negative impression, so there is a growing need to manage one's brand with great care.

Top of the Food Chain

The greatest challenge to global expansion faced by the Mexican cement producer Cemex was to overcome deficiencies in financial resources.

DRIVING FASTER REVENUE GROWTH

The smart company is the one that not only looks ahead, but understands what it sees and makes provision for it. Avon Products CEO Andrea Jung told investors at the 2000 annual Strategic Decisions Conference that the business strategies her company recently adopted have resulted in accelerated revenue growth.

Avon, the world's leading direct seller of beauty and related products with $5.3 billion in annual revenue, markets to women in 137 countries through 3 million field representatives. Jung said that Avon's focus in 2000 was to strengthen its core direct-selling business around the world by investing approximately $100 million to enhance the company's brand image. These efforts included Avon's first-ever global advertising campaign. Highlights of Avon's strategic initiatives included:

• Increasing worldwide advertising spending by 50 percent, including doubling its U.S. advertising budget

• Significant investment to upgrade the quality of sales brochures and offer more free products to customers and representatives

• Moving into new products categories, including the global rollout of its line of jewelry products

• Targeting teen consumers, principally via the Internet, with a new line of products created especially for them

• Launching a B2B Internet strategy to enable E-representatives to sell more productively on-line, using personal Web pages and other business-building tools

Jung said these and certain other initiatives, still in early stages of development, represented potentially significant new revenue streams: "We know that the Avon brand name has the potential to reach new customers in ways we haven't done before, and we are committed to developing those opportunities."[2]

Though it was a low-cost producer, keeping the lid on costs is what spurred its growth in the global market.

Cemex lowered its cost of capital by listing its shares on the New York Stock Exchange, thus tapping international markets. Acquiring two Spanish cement producers allowed the company to shift its financing from short-term Mexican peso debt to longer-term Spanish peseta debt. In addition, it made use of new information technology, a key to succeeding in the logistics-intensive cement industry.

As a result, Cemex is now the world's third largest cement producer, in the category of France's Lafarge, one of its major international competitors. It's also one of the world's lowest-cost producers of cement, having applied the lessons it has learned to boost efficiency in the companies it's acquired. As the *Harvard Business Review* put it: "In the eat-or-be-eaten world of global competition, Cemex is positioning itself at the top of the food chain."[3]

It's always smart to be flexible when market opportunities present themselves—a piece of advice that has too often been ignored by managers in those emerging markets where industrial boundaries have been conventionally and firmly set. Today's more liberal approach to border crossing, exposing companies to various new kinds of competition, should suggest to those managers that they can react effectively by positioning their companies in a variety of ways.

Evolving Global Strategies

As more companies discover how to contend successfully in the global marketplace, we will no doubt see the advent of new and enterprising competitors like Cemex. However, I suspect that many of the most successful companies will still concentrate on local markets to build up their main sources of competitive advantage.

Managers are going to need to reinspect their assumptions as their companies grow. The very nature of their industry may be changing. One company in a basically local business may prosper because of superior service and distribution. But at the same time, a competitor may make moves that change their industry fundamentally, thus giving the advantage to global players.

It has happened before and can again. Some major player raises the ante by developing a superior product at a cost that only a global company with its greater reach can justify. The new manufacturing process drives prices below anything the local producer can sustain.

A Form of Chaos

Today's business growth and future expansion are manifested in a number of ways. Megamergers such as Exxon and Mobil, Travelers Group and Citicorp, Daimler-Benz and Chrysler, America Online and Time Warner, plus major acquisitions such as GE's $45 billion purchase of Honeywell, which had merged with Allied Signal in 1999, proliferate at a staggering rate. It is estimated that there are now more than 200 mergers a week, due largely to the extraordinary abundance of money available for investment.

It's almost a form of chaos on a global level. As the global market expands and interconnectivity increases throughout the world, leaders will be required to handle multidisciplinary tasks, nimbly and creatively. Their horizons will broaden, and their vision must be fixed clearly on the road ahead.

Building a global brand will certainly be one of the key challenges many managers will face in the twenty-first century. As I have stressed, branding codifies a company's identity and can fix its position in the global marketplace. Thus, it becomes imperative for the growth-seeking company to develop its own distinct, international branding strategy and, once established, to communicate and nurture its brand.

The Critical Issue

Kevin Roberts, Saatchi & Saatchi CEO, has written in *Advertising Age* on the future of brands and advertising in a global marketplace:

> The critical issue of the next 100 years of advertising and brands isn't the Internet or market fragmentation . . . [it's] what role will brands play in developing the world and helping individuals lead more enriching lives?
>
> I'm totally positive about the potential for brands, brand management, and the advertising industry to play a central role in building a better world. It won't just happen, though. Traditional brands . . . could be left behind if we keep playing by the same old rules. We will have to broaden

our idea about how we present our messages to consumers, and what the role of a brand is in consumers' lives. . . .

The great brands will be driven by ideas bigger than advertising. Big ideas—simple enough to translate to multiple media and retain relevance to every stakeholder group—that get bigger by their own momentum. . . . [Brands] will become more important as trust marks—sources of identity for people, stories people choose to believe in and that help make sense of a chaotic world."[4]

A New Generation of Leaders

Whether business in an uncertain future can enjoy sustained growth in global markets depends, in great measure, on cultivating innovative CEOs to raise the standards of their companies' brands and lead the troops into action. The corporate brand has never been more important, and that importance can only grow.

Globalization—along with a rapidly multiplying number of products and technologies, greater market segmentation across industries, and larger, more varied customer groups—calls for a new generation of leaders who can handle many tasks and manage companies exponentially more complex and demanding than today's. If a company doubles in size, its management challenges may likely triple or even quadruple.

Above all, the new generation of business leaders must be innovative users of communications, drawing on stronger messaging, branding, and marketing skills. Even CFOs must become corporate branding advocates.

To deal with expanding globalization and worldwide interconnectivity, successful leaders of the future will need to take full advantage of the lightning speed of communications techniques, learning how to use these tools not merely to grow their businesses, but also make them more adroit and flexible.

Tomorrow's leaders will have to assimilate facts and ideas much more rapidly because of the expected volume of data that will be generated. They must develop the necessary skills to work in a globally interconnected—and often convoluted—web of business relationships, mastering the art of determining goals, values, and strategies, and making them understood and accepted by many people with differing backgrounds and viewpoints.

An Upward Spiral

Many of those directly involved with branding anticipate bright prospects for it. I recently interviewed Patrick Gorman, global head of advertising and branding for Ciba Specialty Chemicals. When asked what he saw as the future of corporate branding, Gorman responded: "It's definitely something that's going to become more and more important. The awareness of corporate branding and what it can do for business has been on an upward spiral for the last decade. Even companies that in the past shied away from publicizing their corporate brands now realize that there has to be an understanding of their brands in order to support share price as well as sell products."

Regardless of how well or how poorly their names may be recognized, companies today accept the necessity for recognized global brands. After all, each company is seeking equity from the same places as every other company. When you're up against the GEs and Microsofts, it becomes a real challenge if you or the nature of your business is not known. Don't forget, the value of the brand is just as important to the investment professional as it is to the consumer.

Many of today's mergers cross national boundaries. While most of these currently originate from North America and Western Europe—because that's where the money is—I believe that in the next 20 years more alliances will be formed with companies in Asia, Latin America, and the Middle East. If I'm right, then having a globally recognized name is going to be even more important.

Of the many questions I receive when I lecture, the most frequently raised regard the role of corporate and global branding in the future.

Momentous events are changing the way we think about the world, events that are bringing the world closer together, events that are changing consumer perceptions of products and influencing the choices they make, events that are altering the ways companies do business and compete. And these changes are exerting considerable pressure on companies to develop their own global brands.

Despite these changes—or perhaps because of them—I am convinced that the true value of clear and consistent branding is becoming more widely recognized and embraced by CEOs and senior management of corporations everywhere. The acceptance of branding is sure to have significant impact on the function, structure, and effectiveness of corporate communications.

I also believe that the return on investment (ROI) for corporate communications—a measurement of the communications effect on corporate reputation, and the resulting impact on stock performance—will become a fully accepted accounting principle.

I also see corporate communications departments worldwide being held accountable, and even rewarded, for contributing to corporate financial performance. Communications budgets will be shaped by the outcome—successful or unsuccessful—of ROI expectations.

The Narrowing "Brandwidth"

As I pointed out in Chapter 10, a number of the best known and respected brands have lost some of their glamour. In 1999, for the first time in the 10-year history of Corporate Branding Index (CBI) studies, many highly regarded companies experienced a notable drop in their scores. Eight thousand executives at large U.S. companies were asked to grade 575 corporate brands on familiarity, overall reputation, management strength, and investment potential. Each respondent rated 40 companies, with scores ranging from 1 to 100.

Among the 115 companies with the highest ratings, the average CoreBrand Power score fell 7.7 percent, to 50.9. The second tier companies—numbers 116 to 230—dropped nearly 11 percent, to 28.9 percent. In contrast, the average score for the bottom 115 companies rose about 42 percent, to 10.9 percent. While it is not unusual to see newer or weaker brands leap ahead in the annual Corporate Branding survey, the broad decline among the most powerful brands was startling.

This is an extraordinary finding. Further, we do not believe the CoreBrand Power decline is a onetime phenomenon. Clearly, the rules of branding are changing; now is not the time to become comfortable with your brand's historic position. Old-line companies lost ground in the survey partly because of the ascendancy of the New Economy and many new E-brands clamoring for attention. Today's crowded marketplace has narrowed the perceptual "brandwidth" of consumers and investors, who can cope with only so many brand names.

It is apparent that some of the younger or more obscure companies are judged to be more appealing financial investments these days than the household names. Investment potential, I believe, was the major fac-

	1999	1998	% Change
Quintile 1	50.9	55.2	−7.7%
Quintile 2	28.9	32.4	−10.8%
Quintile 3	19.0	19.5	−2.6%
Quintile 4	14.1	12.5	+12.8%
Quintile 5	10.9	7.7	+41.5%

Figure 12.1 *Corporate Branding Study Compares CoreBrand Power Scores*

tor driving down the favorability ratings of the top-tier companies. A number of consultants, myself included, also believe some companies neglect—or mishandle—their corporate brands. They resort to expedient, knee-jerk reactions, often merely launching another new advertising campaign. In short, more of the same.

A New Kind of Senior Officer

What does all this mean for the future? One is compelled to conclude that branding is now more important than ever to a company's success. Consider the competition for investment dollars in a capital arena with new, and seemingly glamorous, high techs and dot-coms. In this environment, well-executed branding not only builds and reinforces awareness and knowledge of your company, attracting investors as well as customers, but studies show it can improve both share price and return on investment.

Corporate branding can also help open the door to the global marketplace, crossing borders to provide for a viable, decision-making mindset throughout your organization: from marketing to communications to finance to legal, your brand is clearly your most valuable asset.

As you must have noted, I can't stress enough the inclusion of global branding in the list of major responsibilities of a chief executive officer. It is the CEO who has the experience, the leadership, the understanding, and the focus on *all* business facets of his or her company. It is the CEO who has the vision of where the company is heading, understands the circumstances of its drive for globalization, and can project how it's going to get there.

But the CEO, by anyone's definition, is a busy individual with a great many responsibilities for a broad range of activities. Occupied with the many aspects of globalization—as well as with the many other details of the business—the CEO may easily lose sight of one of his or her major missions: the care and maintenance of the global brand.

The fact is that he or she may not have the background necessary for the smooth, effective communication of ideas and plans for global branding. What's more, the CEO is under pressure all the time. Demands on the CEO's time may be so onerous that branding will not get enough of his or her attention—as important to the company's global expansion as the brand may be.

And so I see corporate communications and other brand-related disciplines—advertising, investor relations, public relations, public affairs, human resources, and so forth—coming together under one corporate leadership umbrella. A new kind of senior officer—a chief communications officer (CCO) or chief branding officer (CBO) or chief marketing officer (CMO)—will be created to head the corporate communications department, with responsibility for corporate branding, and with direct access to the CEO and CFO.

It makes good sense. In most other corporate areas, the CEO is given significant support in the form of an experienced senior officer, e.g., a chief financial officer (CFO), chief operations officer (COO), chief administrative officer (CAO), chief information officer (CIO).

This chief communications or branding officer would be vested with more authority than the traditional "logo cop," who is involved chiefly with the details of corporate identity. He or she would have much broader responsibilities, not the least of which would be that of establishing global brand strategy and aligning it with corporate business strategy. This would not diminish the CEO's basic accountability; rather, it would give the CEO a strong, experienced arm to lean on.

Whatever his or her title, the candidate will need broad-based global branding and communications skills and must be able to act as a trained spokesperson for the company. In light of the complexities of communications in the thriving global marketplace, such a new position is particularly desirable. The CEO, of course, would still maintain personal stewardship of the brand, but the CEO is generally far too involved with other aspects of the business to give branding full, day-by-day attention.

Don't Let the Future Just Happen

My main point is that focusing on the future rather than dwelling on the past is crucial for the achievement of success in a global environment. You can't let the future just happen to your company. Change, particularly the kind of change necessitated by globaliziaton, calls upon the CEO, his or her directors and management team, to demonstrate clear vision and steadfast commitment to the corporate/global brand.

Saatchi & Saatchi's Kevin Roberts writes:

> Brands must be more than just a set of attributes with a visual identity. Successful future brands will regard themselves as stories people believe in. The heroes of these stories will be anything—products, services, personalities, even attitudes. . . . Brands will become more important as a source of our personal belief systems. . . . Brands are transforming themselves from fashion statements into articles of faith. Future brands will be more conscious of telling stories that play more directly to our emotions and imaginations. . . .
>
> In almost every global industry, we are in for 100 years of rapid change and uncertainty. . . . But one thing is certain. For the optimistic, the courageous and the imaginative . . . the next 100 years have boundless possibilities."[5]

I, too, firmly believe that the economic possibilities of this new century are limitless. It would not surprise me if eventually the entire world entered the global market—spreading free-market capitalism to virtually every nation. But such times are not for the timid or prosaic. Only with consummate understanding, aggressive imagination, and unyielding nerve can success be achieved.

The world is well on its way, however. This new era of globalization is already fast becoming the dominant international system, replacing, as Thomas L. Friedman points out in *The Lexus and the Olive Tree*, the old Cold War system:

> The Cold War system was characterized by one overarching feature—division. The world was a divided-up, chopped-up place, and both your

threats and opportunities . . . to grow out of who you were divided from. Appropriately, this Cold War system was symbolized by a single word: the *wall*—the Berlin Wall. . . .

The globalization system is a bit different. It also has one overarching feature—integration. The world has become an increasingly interwoven place, and today, whether you are a company or a country, your threats and opportunities increasingly derive from who you are connected to. This globalization system is also characterized by a single word: the *Web*. So in the broadest sense we have gone from a system built around division and walls to a system increasingly built around integration and webs. . . .

The globalization system, unlike the Cold War system, is not frozen, but a dynamic ongoing process. . . . It is the inexorable integration of markets, nation-states, and technologies never witnessed before—in a way that is enabling individuals, corporations, and nation-states to reach around the world farther, faster, deeper, and cheaper than ever before, and in a way that is enabling the world to reach into individuals, corporations, and nation-states farther, faster, deeper, cheaper than ever before.[6]

And as I have already pointed out, the process can also, unfortunately, produce violent repercussions by those broken, abandoned or otherwise outraged by the various effects of globalization.

Predictions are seldom accompanied by guarantees. But if anything is sure, it is this: today's fiercely competitive marketplace will only become more competitive. The company with a courageous vision, the company that can build, communicate, and protect a consistent global corporate brand—while outperforming the competition in its core businesses and capitalizing on the new opportunities it will encounter—is bound to excel in the twenty-first century.

Ten Key Points to Review and Remember

1. Three influential drivers of the twenty-first century economy:
   - Burgeoning information revolution
   - Birth of exciting new industries
   - Expansion of the global marketplace

2. The company that looks to master tomorrow's worldwide markets will find new ways to keep costs down, while making every effort to plan, execute, and communicate a powerful, clear-cut international branding strategy.

3. It's always smart to be flexible when market opportunities present themselves. Managers need to revisit their assumptions and conclusions as the capabilities of their companies develop. Not only will they find their strategies likely to evolve over time, but the very nature of their industries may change as well.

4. As the global marketplace expands and interconnectivity increases throughout the world, leaders will be required to handle multidisciplinary tasks, nimbly and creatively, and make their goals, values, and strategies understood and accepted by many people with different backgrounds and viewpoints.

5. In the next 100 years in an increasingly uncertain information-laden world, brands will become more important as trust marks— sources of identity for people, stories for them to believe in and that help make sense of a chaotic world.

6. Even companies that in the past shied away from publicizing their corporate brands now realize there has to be an understanding of their brands in order to support share price as well as to sell products. It becomes a real challenge if your company or the nature of your business is not known.

7. The acceptance of branding by CEOs and senior management is sure to have significant impact on the function, structure, and effectiveness of corporate communications around the world.

8. Return on investment for corporate communications—a measurement of the communications effect on corporate reputation and the resulting impact on stock performance—should become a fully accepted accounting principle, with communications budgets shaped by the outcome of ROI expectations.

9. Corporate communications and other brand-related disciplines should come together under one corporate leadership umbrella. A new kind of senior officer, a chief communications officer (CCO) or chief

branding officer (CBO), should be created to give the CEO significant support in the branding area and have direct access to the CEO and CFO.

10. The ability to focus on the future rather than dwell on the past is crucial for success in a global environment. The possibilities of this new century seem limitless, but these times are not for the timid or prosaic. The company with vision, that can communicate a consistent global corporate brand while outperforming competition in core businesses and capitalizing on new opportunities, is bound to excel.

Selected Reading List

Aaker, David A., and Erich Joachimsthaler. *Brand Leadership*. New York: The Free Press, Division of Simon & Schuster, Inc., 2000.

Bryan, Lowell, Jane Fraser, Jeremy Oppenheim, and Wilhem Rall. *Race for the World: Strategies to Build a Great Global Firm.* Boston: Harvard Business School Press, 1999.

Dauphinais, G. William, and Colin Price, editors. Price Waterhouse. *Straight from the CEO*. New York: Simon & Schuster, 1998.

Friedman, Thomas L. *The Lexus and the Olive Tree*. New York: Farrar, Straus and Giroux, 1999.

Gregory, James R., with Jack G. Wiechmann. *Leveraging the Corporate Brand*. Chicago: NTC/Contemporary Publishing Group Inc., 1997.

Gregory, James R., with Jack G. Wiechmann. *Marketing Corporate Image: The Company as Your Number One Product*. Second Edition. Chicago: NTC/Contemporary Publishing Group, Inc., 1999.

Higgins, Richard B. *The Search for Corporate Strategic Credibility: Concepts and Cases in Global Strategy Communications*. Westport, CT: Quorum Books, 1996.

Klein, Naomi. *No Logo: Taking Aim at the Brand Bullies*. New York: Picador USA, 1999.

Micklethwait, John, and Adrian Wooldridge. *A Future Perfect: The Essentials of Globalization.* Crown Business: New York, 2000.

Moran, Robert T., and John R. Riesenberger. *The Global Challenge: Building the New Worldwide Enterprise.* London: McGraw-Hill International (UK) Limited, 1994.

Schultz, Don E., and Jeffrey S. Walters. *Measuring Brand Communication ROI.* New York: Association of National Advertisers, Inc., 1997.

Temporal, Paul. *Branding in Asia: The Creation, Development and Management of Asian Brands for the Global Market.* Singapore: John Wiley & Sons (Asia) Pte Ltd, 1999.

Notes

Introduction

1. James P. Kelly, "Growing a Global Delivery System," The Conference Board, Vol. 1, No. 4, 1997

2. Iain Somerville, "The Global Dimension," *CEO Report*, Anderson Consulting World Forum on Change

3. G. William Dauphinais and Colin Price, "Globalization," *Straight from the CEO* (Simon & Schuster, 1998), 24

Chapter 1

1. Shelly Lazarus, remarks made in presentation to Asia Corporate Branding Symposium, Singapore, February 24, 2000

2. Mukul Pandya, "A Good Brand Is Hard to Buy," *Wall Street Journal*, June 9, 2000

3. James P. Kelly, "Growing a Global Delivery System," The Conference Board, Vol. 1, No. 4, 1997, 15–20

4. Ibid.

5. Mukul Pandya, op. cit.

6. Edwina Woodbury, "To the Ends of the Earth," *CEO Report*, Anderson Consulting World Forum on Change, 13

7. Dr. Christopher M. Miller and Lindsey Michaels, "Global Brand Management," *Thunderbird*, The American Graduate School of International Management, Vol. 53, No. 1, 1999

8. Kathryn Troy, "Managing the Corporate Brand," The Conference Board, Research Report 1214–98–RR

9. Ibid.

10. Ibid.

11. Clark Johnson, "Preserving the Trade," *Chief Executive*, April 1998, 43–44

12. Troy, "Managing the Corporate Brand," op. cit.

13. Melissa A. Berman, "How CEOs Drive Global Growth," The Conference Board, Report No. 1184–97–RR

Chapter 2

1. Chris Macrae (editor), "Cadbury Schweppes Character Source," *MELNET*, Interview with Sir Adrian Cadbury, 1989

2. "What Is ITT?," *Reputation Management*, November/December 1998, 66–68

Chapter 4

1. Gail Edmondson, et. al., "The Beauty of Global Branding," *Business Week*, June 28, 1999, 70–75

2. Peter Levin, "Creating a Higher Standard . . ." *Thunderbird*, The American Graduate School of International Management, Vol. 53, No. 1, 1999

3. Allen Freedman, "Values, Culture & Global Effectiveness," CE Roundtable, *Chief Executive*, April 1998, 51–61

4. Jacques R. Chevron, "Global Branding: Married to the World," *Advertising Age*, May 15, 1995

5. Jürgen Dormann, "The Challenges of Globalization," *Global Finance*, June 1999, 20

6. Peter Galuszka, Ellen Neuborne, Wendy Zellner, "P&G's Hottest New Product: P&G," *Business Week*, October 5, 1998, 92–96

7. Keith Bradsher, "A Struggle Over Culture and Turf at Auto Giant," *New York Times*, September 25, 1999

8. "Making 'Digital' Decisions—DaimlerChrysler Chief Explains His Tough Calls," *Wall Street Journal*, September 24, 1999

9. Dana Mead, "A Different Country, A Different Calculus" *CEO Report*, Anderson Consulting World Forum on Change, 1998, 16

10. Alisa Tang, "The Global Ceiling?" *New York Times*, Business Section, September 12, 1999, 12

11. Dana Mead, "The Global Gamble," *Chief Executive*, January/February 1998, 27

12. Brandon Mitchener, "Border Crossings," *Wall Street Journal*, November 22, 1999, R41

13. Ronald E. Berenbeim, "Global Corporate Ethics Practices: A Developing Consensus," *Chief Executive Digest*, Vol. 3, No. 3, 1999, 22–25

Chapter 5

1. Nitin Nohria, "The War for Global Talent," *CEO Report*, Anderson Consulting, 16

2. David A. Light, "Pioneering Distance Education in Africa," *Harvard Business Review*, September–October 1999, 26

3. James Kelly, chairman and CEO, UPS, taken from remarks made before the Johns Hopkins University School of Business and Education, www.prnewswire.com, March 2, 2000

4. Lowell L. Bryan, Jane Fraser, Jeremy Oppenheim, Wilhelm Rall, *Race for the World: Strategies to Build a Great Global Firm* (Harvard Business School Press, 1999), 141

5. Michael J. Mandel, "The New Economy," *Business Week*, January 31, 2000, 73–77

6. Julie Moline, "Paying for Expats," *Global Finance*, April 1999, 64

7. W. Wayne Allen, "An HR Strategy for Asia-Pacific Operations," *Chief Executive Digest*, The Conference Board, Vol. 3, No. 3, 1999, 5–9

8. Minoru Murofushi, "An Agile Giant," *Straight from the CEO*, G. William Dauphinais and Colin Price, editors (Simon & Schuster, 1998), 60–64

Chapter 6

1. Alex Taylor III, "Detroit Goes Digital," *Fortune*, April 17, 2000, 170–74

2. Spencer E. Ante and Arlene Weintraub, "Why B2B Is a Scary Place to Be," *Business Week*, September 11, 2000, 34–37

3. "Stock Exchanges. The Battle for Efficient Markets," *The Economist*, June 17, 2000, 69–71

4. Marc Gunther, "These Guys Want It All," *Fortune*, February 7, 2000, 71–78

5. Sarah Ellison, "Web-Brand Study Says Awareness Isn't Trust," *Wall Street Journal*, June 7, 2000, B2

6. Caroline McNally, "Corporate Image Strategies," *Conference Highlights* The Conference Board Europe, November 16–17, 1999

7. Philip Evans and Thomas S. Wurster, "Getting Real About Virtual Commerce," *Harvard Business Review*, November–December 1999, 85–94

8. Stephen Baker, Irene M. Kunii, and Steven V. Brull, "Here Come Smart Phones," *Business Week*, October 25, 1999, 167–78

9. "Telecommunications: The World in Your Pocket," survey, *The Economist,* October 9, 1999, 5–36

10. Randall Poe and Carol Lee Courter, "Selling It on the Web," *Across the Board*, July/August 1999, 5

11. Gene Koprowski, "A Brief History of Web Advertising," *Critical Mass*, Fall 1999, 8–14

12. Philip Clark, "Citibank Will Host Global Biz Web Sites," *Ad Age International*, September 1999, 1, 4

13. "Digital Bridge to Participate in U.S. Trade Mission. . . .," *AOL News*, June 8, 2000

14. Jonathon Moore and Bruce Einhorn, "A Business-to-Business E-Boom," *Business Week*, October 25, 1999, 62

Chapter 7

1. Paul Temporal, *Branding in Asia*, (John Wiley & Sons [Asia] Pte Ltd., 1999), 201–202

2. Eva Zaeschmar, "Unleashing the Power of the Reuters Brand," *Investor's Newsletter*, reuters.com, June 1998

3. Mike Koller, "HP's Fiorina Delivers Vision of Internet Future," *Internet Week Online*, November 15, 1999

4. "Enhancing Brand Value for Shell," A Promptu Customer Case Study, June 10, 2000

5. John Evan Frook, "Shell Goes Online for Global Brand Control," *BtoB*, April 10, 2000, 6, 51

6. "Enhancing Brand Value for Shell," op. cit.

7. John Evan Frook, op. cit.

8. Don Argus, "Focusing Leadership Through Corporate Values," *Straight from the CEO*, G. William Dauphinais and Colin Price, editors (Simon & Schuster, 1998), 199–206

9. Ibid.

10. Sue Zesigner, "Jac Nasser Is Car Crazy," *Fortune*, June 22, 1998, 79–82

11. Kathryn Troy, "The Essentials of Brand Management," *Managing the Corporate Brand*, Research Report 1214–98–RR, 22–23

Chapter 8

1. Gianpaolo Caccini, "Lessons from the Front," *Chief Executive*, June 2000, 43–46

2. Ronald E. Ferguson, "Leading the Way" letter to corporate colleagues, promotional booklet for GeneralCologneRe, 2000.

3. David Fairlamb and Stanley Reed, "Über Bank," *Business Week*, March 20, 2000, 52–53

4. Debra Sparks "Partners," *Business Week*, October 25, 1999, 106–12

5. Gerald Greenwald, "Tracking an Alliance's Takeoff," *Chief Executive Digest*, Vol. 3, No. 3, 1999, 11–14

6. Melanie Trottman, "Airline Alliance Is Set to Form Online Market," *Wall Street Journal*, April 28, 2000, B2

Chapter 9

1. Lucy Alexander and Sigrid Esser, "Globalizing the Board of Directors: Trends and Strategies," *Chief Executive Digest*, Vol. 3, No. 3, 1999, 18–21

2. Lucy Alexander and Sigrid Esser, "Best Practices in Recruiting Non-National Directors," The Conference Board, Research Report 1242–99–RR, 18–23

3. Carolyn Kay Brancato, "Communicating Corporate Performance: A Delicate Balance," The Conference Board, Special Report No. 1, 45

4. Robert Lear, "Twenty Years of Corporate Governance—from the Director's Chair," *Chief Executive*, August 1997, 16

5. Ronald E. Berenbeim, "Global Corporate Ethics Practices: A Developing Consensus," *Chief Executive Digest*, Vol. 3, No. 3, 1999, 22–25

6. Carolyn Kay Brancato, op. cit., 73

7. Julie Daum, "Women on Board," *Chief Executive*, October 1998, 40–43

8. Ibid.

Chapter 10

1. Juliana Koranteng, et al., "Coke Marshals Forces After Crisis in Europe," *Ad Age International*, July 1999, 3

2. William Echikson and Dean Foust, "For Coke, Local Is It," *Business Week*, July 3, 2000, 122

3. James Brandman and Kathryn Hanes, "Branding the World," *Global Finance*, March 31, 2000, 50–51

4. Scott Kilman and Thomas M. Burton, "Monsanto Boss's Vision of 'Life Sciences' Firm Now Confronts Reality," *Wall Street Journal*, December 21, 1999, A1, A10

5. Ibid.

6. Roger Cohen, "Fearful Over the Future, Europe Seizes on Food," *New York Times*, August 29, 1999

7. Louise Lee, "Can Nike Still Do It?" *Business Week*, February 21, 2000, 120–128

8. Jeffrey E. Garten, "CEOs: Prepare for More Protests," *Wall Street Journal*, December 6, 1999

9. Ibid.

10. Paul Magnusson, "Meet Free Traders' Worst Nightmare," *Business Week*, March 20, 2000, 113–18

11. James Ledbetter, "Brand Names," *New York Times Book Review*, April 23, 2000

12. Keith Kirby, CEO, Elmwood Co., "No Logo, No Substance." *The Journal of Brand Management*, Vol. 8, No. 1, September 2000, 77–78

Chapter 11

1. Teri Ross, "Digital Asset Management: The Art of Archiving," techexchange.com, June 1999

2. Jeff Kaufman, from Cirqit.com press releases, July 13, 2000 and October 5, 2000

Chapter 12

1. Gerald Greenwald, "Tracking an Alliance's Takeoff," *Chief Executive Digest*, Vol. 3, No. 3, 1999, 11–14

2. "Avon Says Business Strategies Are Driving Faster Revenue Growth," *AOL News*, June 7, 2000

3. Niraj Dawar and Tony Frost, "Competing with Giants," *Harvard Business Review*, March–April 1999, 119–29

4. Kevin Roberts "Brand Identity 2000: Redefining the World," *Advertising Age*, November 29, 1999, 50

5. Kevin Roberts, op. cit.

6. Thomas L. Friedman, *The Lexus and the Olive Tree* (Anchor Books, Random House, Inc., 2000; originally published by Farrar, Straus and Giroux, 1999)

Credits

Index